I0750983

Kingdom

Explorations of the Sermon on the Mount

David T. Noland

A Seedroar Ministries Publication

KINGDOM: *Explorations of the Sermon on the Mount*
By David T. Noland

Cover Design: Author
Interior Design: Author

ISBN:

978-1-326-30101-9
First Edition, 2026

For information, inquiries, or permissions, contact:
David T. Noland – dnoland72@gmail.com

Table of Contents

To my bride Sara, our children, and our grandchildren:

May our own small "kingdom"

never outshine the eternal Kingdom

for which God has called us to race Heavenward for.

Dedicated to the memory
of our dearly departed sister in Christ,

Brenda Gloria

Who not only represented the Kingdom well,
but demonstrated the Kingdom
with immeasurable grace every day of her life.

Acknowledgements

Nothing ever worth doing is easy and writing is no exception. It requires time and patience, but most importantly it requires prayer and partnership. No journey in this life is complete without the guidance, assistance, and companionship that comes with friends and fellow citizens of the Kingdom.

This study began in my own personal quiet time years ago and was originally published on my former blog, which has since been shut down. I wanted to understand the implications of the Kingdom principles of God's Word and I thought what better place to start than at the very beginning of Jesus' ministry as He heralded the arrival of the Kingdom. I was not disappointed. What follows here is merely the beginning of a lifelong journey of transformation, identity, discipleship, and mission that ultimately will culminate in the consummation of the Kingdom as we walk through Heaven's Gate in the fullness of time.

Along the way, I've been blessed to know many who have been mentors and have prayed for me, not knowing about this project. Their hands of leadership and guidance and encouragement have been immeasurable.

First and foremost, thanks is reserved for King Jesus as He is the only one worthy of my highest gratitude and praise. Of the lengthy list of mentors that have influenced my life and pursuit of theology, His influence outshines them all.

I wish to thank my pastor, Dr. Danny Forshee for your leadership of Great Hills Baptist Church and for inspiring me towards discipleship and mission as a singular endeavor. Missions is the goal of discipleship; discipleship is incomplete without the pursuit of the Great Commission.

To my professors at Southwestern Baptist Theological Seminary – Dr. Jeffrey Bingham, Dr. Ted Cabal, Dr. Jon Okinaga, Dr. Chris Osborne, Dr. Dean Sieberhagen, Dr. Jim

Wicker, Dr. Michael Wilkinson, and Dr. Malcolm Yarnell. I have studied at the feet of giants among men, of which you humbly shall always be counted as chief among them.

To my partner in life, Sara. You are my "ezer kenegdo", my suitable helper whom God created for me to be everything that I am not. You strengthen me when I am weak and you shine when life is at its darkest.

Finally, to you the reader. Thank you for taking the time to pick up this humble tome and trusting me to be your guide through the kingdom that God calls us to represent as citizens, ambassadors, and apostles. I do not take lightly the responsibility that is placed on my shoulders to guide you. Grace and peace belong to you as you begin this journey.

By His grace,

David T. Noland

The Manifesto of the Kingdom

"Seeing the crowds, he [Jesus] went up on the mountain, and when he sat down, his disciples came to him. And he open his mouth and taught them…" Matthew 5:1-2

The word "manifesto" often carries with it a bit of a negative connotation, largely due to its association with "The Communist Manifesto" and the various mission statements of certain serial criminals and terrorists. However, by definition, a manifesto is a bold, public declaration of convictions and intentions designed to *inspire action*, *define purpose*, and *challenge the status quo*. It unites belief with urgency and aims to shape the future. As a result, this definition would encompass such documents as the Declaration of Independence or the US Constitution.

Generally a manifesto contains seven elements: a clear purpose or vision, core beliefs or convictions, a call to action, a tone of urgency or boldness, defined opposition, communal orientation, or a moral/theological framework. While the Sermon on the Mount is not generally a "political" statement, is does meet the requirements of the definition provided above as a verbally publicly delivered statement of "intention, motives, and views of its issuer" and contains all the described elements.

The Sermon on the Mount was Jesus first clear extended statement of purpose related to the Kingdom of Heaven. The gospel writer Matthew makes this a key theme throughout his writing. It is the first extended teaching that Matthew records, and as the first it is positioned to be the most important of His teachings upon which the rest of the gospel of Matthew illustrates. While the text itself doesn't explicitly declare the exact location of where the sermon is delivered, we do know that it was in the region of Galilee in the north of Israel, as Jesus returned from the regions of Syria, Jordan, and the Decapolis because we are told exactly that in the text in Matthew 4:25.

This book is designed to be a 40-day study as you carefully and methodically walk through Jesus' kingdom manifesto of the Sermon on the Mount. It will contain a reading from the biblical text and attempt to illuminate the words of Jesus and provide you with insight into His meaning within the 1st century context of the original hearers of the sermon and the original readers of the text as recorded by Matthew as an eyewitness to the sermon.

Each day's readings will be followed by a series of Reflection Questions, Application Points, and a Prayer Prompt to guide your mediation of the text of Scripture. It is my hope and my prayer that you will dive deep into the text and fully grasp what Jesus is trying to say to the people He was sent to redeem and welcome into the Kingdom.

The text used in the study is from the English Standard Version, but you as the reader are welcome to use an alternative Biblical text for your own reading that helps your understanding of the text. Feel free to take notes in the provided spaces.

Above all, I pray by the end of this study, you will have been drawn closer to the Lord of life. If you do not have a personal relationship with Jesus, I urge you to reach out to someone you know that is a Christian and ask them questions about this book. Have them walk through it with you. If you want to know more about what it means to know and follow Jesus, you can reach out to the good folks at Need Him Global (needhim.org) and start an online chat conversation with one of their agents who will be happy to answer any questions you have about matters of faith in Christ.

Grace and peace be unto you as you begin this journey of faith in the Kingdom of Jesus.

The Gospel of the Kingdom

"And He went throughout all Galilee, teaching in their synagogues and proclaiming the gospel of the kingdom and healing every disease and every affliction among the people. So His fame spread throughout all Syria, and they brought Him all the sick, those afflicted with various diseases and pains, those oppressed by demons, those having seizures, and paralytics, and He healed them. And great crowds followed Him from Galilee and the Decapolis, and from Jerusalem and Judea, and from beyond the Jordan." (Matthew 4:23-25)

What is this "Gospel"?

All too often, we have a tendency in translating to the English language to simplify concepts, perhaps oversimplify, and in so doing, we lose some of the intended meaning of the original composition. The Greek work "euangelion" which we translate as "gospel" does indeed translate to "good news," however there is a historical nuance that we miss that is directly related to the declaration of the arrival of the Kingdom of God.

Historically, the word "euangelion" was used to announce the good news that a new king has arrived, and with him, a new kingdom. Generally this message was delivered by an appointed "euangelistou," or evangelist, whose job was not only to announce the imminent arrival of the new king, but they were also responsible for preparing the pathway for the king's arrival. As such, John the Baptizer would be considered the original evangelist of the Kingdom as he echoes the words of the prophet Isaiah when he proclaims, "The voice of one crying in the wilderness, 'Prepare the way of the Lord; make his paths straight." (Matthew 3:3)

In such cases, the imagery that Isaiah was presenting was that of a highway being cleared in the desert to prepare for the arrival of the King that was coming to redeem His people. In the case of John the Baptizer, he was announcing the King has indeed arrived. And his quoting of Isaiah was not lost on the religious leaders of his day as it was the first rumblings of "trouble" in the hearts of the established religious rulers.

The Citizens of the Kingdom

Was Jesus there to teach the Jews and point them to God and proclaim His kingdom on earth? Yes. Did He come to heal the sick, cure pain, cast out demons, comfort the oppressed? Yes. Did He come to minister to the religious Jewish community? Yes. Did He come to minister beyond the confines of religious and national boundaries? Absolutely yes!

As far back as the very beginning of Jesus' ministry, following His forty days in the wilderness to be tempted by Satan, He did not restrict His movements to just the religiously and nationally acceptable regions of Israel.

The Reach of the Kingdom

He was known throughout all of Syria, a Gentile region north of Israel that extended as far north as modern Turkey and western Armenia and as far east as the modern northwestern border of Iran, encompassing part of what is now northernmost Iraq, due north of Baghdad.

Just across the Jordan River, outside of Israel proper, was a region known as the Decapolis, in the modern day kingdom of Jordan. The Decapolis was a group of ten cities that marked the easternmost boundary of the Roman Empire in that day: Gerasa, Scythopolis, Hippos, Gadara, Pella, Philadelphia (now Amman, the capital of Jordan), Capitolias, Canatha, Raphana, and Damascus (the modern day capital of Syria). Damascus was a major trading post at the crossroads of Europe, Asia, and Palestine on the western edge along the centralized north-south Mediterranean coast portion of what is known as the Fertile Crescent.

In Gerasa, there is an oval forum, a place that was surrounded by large stone columns with a column lined pathway that leads to the forum. Much like the Roman Forum in the capitol of the Empire, the Gerasene Forum was a center for trade, political discourse, education, oratory, and much more. In the center of the forum is a small column, providing a point of reference for those within the forum. If you wanted the news of the day, this is where you get it. If you were to look closely at the layout of the Gerasene Forum, it may appear very familiar in design to you. Speculation suggests that this design may have inspired Michaelangelo as he designed the architecture of St. Peter's Basilica and the rotunda that leads up to it as it was representative of the designs of the forums across the ancient Roman Empire for the exchange of ideas.

The Mission of the King

Jesus didn't come to minister only to the Jews. He intentionally went to the Gentiles outside of Israel. He traveled outside of Galilee to Syria and throughout the Decapolis of Jordan. He taught and He ministered to those who were not those of the Hebrew tribes because He proclaimed "the gospel of the kingdom." When Jesus was challenged by Pilate, He explained that His kingdom was "not of this world." (John 18:36) It was a kingdom that extended beyond the geopolitical constructs of modern man. It was a kingdom that encompassed all who would place their trust in Him and in the Father. And He embraced those that had enough faith in Him to travel from the farthest reaches of the Roman Empire to seek Him and His mercy.

In the same way, the Kingdom of God today extends beyond the walls of our church buildings. It extends beyond the geopolitical confines of our modern world. Jesus extends the Kingdom to the entire world. How dare we ever restrict access to the Kingdom to just those with whom we are comfortable! How dare we restrict access to Jesus to only those who think like us, look like us, or act like us! That's the entire point of the transformative power of grace!

Kingdom Responsibility

We are called to send out the invitation to the dinner table and open the doors to all who will come. We are called to be His ambassadors to a world that needs Him the most. We are called to bring in the broken, the maligned, the sick, the hurting. We are called to be healers for a hurting world. We are called to be teachers to those who are ignorant of the truth. We are called to be an instrument of change, not a trumpet of judgement.

Don't get me wrong. Yes, this message is intended directly for those who believe. Yes, the gospel demands repentance. It demands transformation. Holiness demands obedience to the dictates of God's Word. But for those who have not yet entered the Kingdom, the message is simple: "Come to the table!" Come and see this Savior who can make the lame walk, the blind see, the sick well, the dead live again. Come and see this Savior who can make broken hearts whole and lives renewed. Yes! Repentance is crucial and a part of the gospel message, but it is not the entirety of the gospel message. Grace is the gospel of the kingdom. Mercy is the gift of the kingdom. Transformation is the mission of the kingdom.

"Open your eyes, and see the fields are white for harvest!" (John 4:35) Now is the time. Here is the place. There is no better place to be. There is no greater time than now to let the message of the Kingdom ring loud and clear! The world can be a better place. And it begins in the humble, repentant heart of everyone who seeks Jesus trusting Him to make our lives whole again. It begins with every believer, humbly repenting of their arrogance and bowing on their face before our holy God and say "Not my will, but yours be done."

Reflection Question

- In what ways have I limited the reach of the Kingdom by my assumptions or preferences? How can I better reflect the open-hearted mission of Christ?

  ____

  ____

  ____

Application Points

1. Identify one person outside your usual circles to pray for and reach out to with the gospel.

   ____

   ____

   ____

2. Reflect on the ways your church can better represent the inclusive heart of Christ's Kingdom.

   ____

   ____

   ____

3. Meditate on Matthew 4:23–25 and pray for a heart like Jesus—compassionate, courageous, and kingdom-minded.

Prayer Prompt

"Lord Jesus, You proclaimed the good news of the Kingdom and welcomed the hurting, the outsider, and the lost. Give me Your heart for the world. Help me to be a faithful ambassador—bold in truth, gentle in love, and eager to see Your Kingdom come. Break down the walls in my heart and in my community that hinder Your mission. Amen."

The Poverty of the Kingdom

"Seeing the crowds, he went up on the mountain, and when he sat down, his disciples came to him. And he opened his mouth and taught them, saying: "Blessed are the poor in spirit, for theirs is the kingdom of heaven." Matthew 5:1-3

Crowds had gathered from all over—some from Damascus, a wealthy city along the Fertile Crescent; others from Galilee, a busy fishing region along the Sea of Galilee; and still others from the Decapolis, ten cities beyond the Jordan River in the eastern Roman Empire. People came from far and wide, bringing the sick, the oppressed, and the paralyzed in hopes that the stories of a miracle worker were true. And Jesus healed them.

Then He spoke.

"Blessed are the poor in spirit, for theirs is the kingdom of heaven."

These words must have stirred confusion. What joy could possibly be found in poverty? How could Jesus say those who lacked even the basics of life were "blessed"? In a crowd likely filled with both the rich and the destitute, His message must have turned heads and hearts.

The Real Meaning of "Blessed"

The word "blessed" in this context doesn't simply mean "happy." According to the Hebrew-Greek Key Word Study Bible, the Koine Greek word here is *makarios*, which infers "possessing the characteristics of deity."[1] It's not about wealth, comfort, or emotion—it's about being rightly related to God and finding one's identity in Him.

Jesus wasn't romanticizing poverty or condemning wealth. Rather, He was pointing to something deeper: spiritual humility. Those who recognize their total dependence on God—

who know their spiritual bankruptcy apart from Him—are the ones who belong to His kingdom.

Wealth Cannot Save

Imagine the reactions of the wealthy in the crowd. Some may have scoffed. Others might have quietly looked at their less fortunate neighbors with new eyes. Was Jesus really saying that wealth can't buy access to heaven? Yes, absolutely.

Money can pay for medicine or therapy, but it cannot purchase healing. Only God can bring true restoration. Salvation, healing, and citizenship in God's kingdom cannot be bought—they are given freely by grace through faith in Jesus Christ.

Equal Ground at the Cross

Jesus' words flatten every social structure. The rich and the poor, the healthy and the broken, the educated and the unlearned—all stand on equal ground before God. Earthly status has no bearing on our heavenly standing.

It's not where you come from, what you've done, or who you know that matters. What matters is whether Jesus knows you.

Later in this same sermon, Jesus warns:

"On that day many will say to me, 'Lord, Lord, did we not prophesy in your name...?' And then I will declare to them, 'I never knew you; depart from me...'" (Matthew 7:22–23)

Knowing about Jesus is not enough. Do you know Him personally? And even more importantly—**does He know you**?

The Example of Isaiah

In Isaiah 6, the prophet sees a vision of the Lord. Overwhelmed by God's holiness, he cries:

"Woe is me! For I am lost; for I am a man of unclean lips..." (Isaiah 6:5)

This confession led to cleansing:

"Then one of the seraphim flew to me... and he touched my mouth and said: 'Behold, this has touched your lips; your guilt is taken away, and your sin atoned for.'" (Isaiah 6:6–7)

Isaiah's humility opened the door to forgiveness and purpose. In the same way, when we humbly admit our need, God meets us with grace. Through the sacrifice of Jesus on the cross, we are cleansed, forgiven, and accepted into His kingdom.

True Riches in Christ

There is no greater joy than the joy of being fully known and fully loved by God. When we come to Him with nothing, He gives us everything: forgiveness, identity, purpose, and authority as His children. That is the blessing of being "poor in spirit."

He takes our spiritual poverty and clothes us in the riches of His kingdom.

That's something worth celebrating!

"Blessed are the poor in spirit, for theirs is the kingdom of heaven."

—

Footnote:

1. *Hebrew-Greek Key Study Bible (NASB), ed. Zodhiates, Spiros; Baker, Warren; Kletzing, Joel. AMG Publishers, 1984/1990.*

Reflection Question

- Where have I been trusting in my abilities, reputation, or resources instead of relying fully on God?

  ____

  ____

  ____

Application Points

- Confess an area of pride or self-reliance to God. Ask for His grace to walk in humility.

  ____

  ____

  ____

- **Reach out** to someone who is spiritually broken or discouraged. Offer them encouragement in Christ.

  ____

  ____

  ____

- **Meditate** on Matthew 5:3 this week. Pray for a heart that is poor in spirit but rich in grace.

Prayer Prompt

"Father, I confess that apart from You, I have nothing. But in Christ, I have all I need. Thank You for blessing those who know their need for You. Help me to live in humility, walk in grace, and offer hope to others. Make me truly poor in spirit, so I may be rich in Your kingdom. Amen."

The Mourning of the Kingdom

"Blessed are those who mourn, for they shall be comforted." Matthew 5:4

A Time to Mourn

The month of May is a difficult month for me in a variety of ways. From 2020-2023, our family experienced a string of devastating losses. My grandfather passed away from a very short stint with stomach cancer in May 2020. In May 2021, my father-in-law passed away. In 2023, my youngest brother – a decades long addict – succumb to his addiction as his heart gave out. Within months, my father was diagnosed with lung cancer and his treatments led to a heart attack in December of the same year.

It was an excruciatingly painful season of extended mourning that came in waves. Just as we got our footing back under us, another wave would crash in. However, it was through the loving words and kind gestures of family and friends that we were able to come out on the other side of those times.

Mourning is not an enjoyable experience, but it is a necessary one. That is why Jewish law made it so imperative that people have a time of mourning for the passing of a loved one. The time period for mourning is somewhat flexible, where it is typically seven days, but in some cases (such as with Moses and Aaron) it can be extended to 30 days. According to the laws, a person had to be buried the same day of death and then the mourning period would begin. A meal would be provided and mourners would remain with the family for the entirety of the mourning period to help serve one another and comfort each other during the time of loss.

The Attitude of Mourning

In the second Beatitude, "Blessed are those who mourn, for they shall be comforted," Jesus speaks primarily of a deep sorrow over sin—a godly grief that leads to repentance (cf. 2 Corinthians 7:10). While there are cultural echoes of Jewish mourning practices in the background, Jesus redirects the focus to a spiritual mourning: the heartfelt lament over our sinfulness and the brokenness of the world. This mourning is not merely emotional but is rooted in a recognition of our need for grace. When we come to faith in Christ, we grieve over our former way of life and rejoice in the new life we receive by His mercy.

"Blessed be the God and Father of our Lord Jesus Christ, the Father of mercies and God of all comfort, who comforts us in all our affliction, so that we may be able to comfort those who are in any affliction, with the comfort with which we ourselves are comforted by God. For as we share abundantly in Christ's sufferings, so through Christ we share abundantly in comfort too." *(2 Corinthians 1:3-5)*

The Posture of Mourning

In the Christian life, we will still experience the pain of mourning our sin as we die to our old selves daily to walk in the Light of Christ. But it is in our mourning that we find His comfort. It is in grieving our sinful past that He delights in wrapping His gracious arms about our hearts. It is in the act of daily repentance that we find His peace reigning in our lives.

As we mourn our sin and turn from our old life, we open our hearts to the comfort that God graciously gives to the repentant. Repentance is more than sorrow – it is a Spirit-empowered turning from sin and a reorientation of our hearts toward Christ. Mourning over sin reveals a heart awakened to God's holiness and our need for grace. In that holy grief, the Father meets us – not to shame us, but to fill us with His Spirit, bringing comfort, peace, and healing. You can rest in Him, knowing that He is the God of all comfort, who lifts the brokenhearted, strengthens the weary, and makes your heart beat with new life again.

Reflection Questions

- What does mourning over sin look like in your personal walk with Christ?

  ____

  ____

  ____

- In what areas of your life is the Holy Spirit inviting you to grieve and turn from sin?

  ____

  ____

  ____

- How have you experienced God's comfort in seasons of sorrow or repentance?

  ____

  ____

  ____

Application Points

- Identify a specific sin in your life that the Holy Spirit is prompting you to mourn and repent of. Write it down and confess it before God.

  ____

  ____

  ____

- Consider how your church or small group can create a space of comfort for those who are grieving—spiritually or emotionally.

____

____

____

- Memorize Matthew 5:4 and recite it during your daily prayer time, meditating on its promise of comfort.

____

____

____

Prayer Prompt

Heavenly Father, I come to You with a heart that grieves over my sin and the brokenness around me. Thank You for the comfort that You promise to those who mourn. Help me to walk in daily repentance, and may Your Spirit heal and renew my heart. Use my sorrow to draw me closer to You and equip me to comfort others with the same grace You've shown me. In Jesus' name, Amen.

The Meekness of the Kingdom

"Blessed are the meek, for they shall inherit the earth." Matthew 5:5

The first time I ever heard the word "meek" was in that classic childhood film "The Wizard of Oz." Dorothy stood before the fearsome visage of the Wizard who thunders: "I am Oz - the Great and Powerful. Who are you? Who are you?!" Dorothy's timid response was "If you please, I am Dorothy - the small and meek. We've come to ask -- " And then she is rudely cut off by the potentate of the Emerald City with a loud "SILENCE!"

Rethinking Meekness

The image of meekness portrayed here is one of comparative weakness. Dorothy's small frame and stature compared to the authoritative and strong Wizard. But when Jesus says, "Blessed are the meek", what sounds like a paradox is in fact not so much. The Greek word that is translated as "meek" is **πραΰς**. Contextually, it expresses a grace of the soul that is more akin to gentleness. Furthermore, in Scripture the word is used to demonstrate an attitude of **not being overly impressed by a sense of one's self-importance**.

So what does that mean in the context of the Beatitudes and Jesus' allusion to inheritance? Remember, the Biblical term for "blessed" is representative of God's approval and the impartation of His authority upon His children. As we grow in our faith, we learn that one of the fruit of the Spirit is "gentleness" (Galatians 5:22-23). As the fruit of the Spirit are developed elements of individual character within each believer, we demonstrate these virtues in our actions and attitudes with the world around us. In so doing, we are fulfilling our sacred responsibilities as "ambassadors of Christ" (2 Corinthians 5:20) and His Kingdom. As adopted children of our Abba Father, redeemed by the blood of His Son, and sealed by His Holy Spirit, we are entitled to the inheritance of His Kingdom as sons and daughters of the Most High God.

Ambassadors with Authority

So ultimately, what Jesus is saying here is this: Because we are His ambassadors, we are imparted a sense of authority during our time on Earth. But we are expected to exercise that authority with gentleness. We are not called to brow beat the gospel into people. We are not called to wield our Bibles as royal scepters. We have been sent out "like sheep in the midst of wolves, so be wise as serpents, but gentle as doves." (Matthew 10:16)

Therefore, meekness is a character trait of genuine, spiritual authority. It is a humble recognition of our position before the Almighty God, but a confident acknowledgement that we are children of our Creator. It is a gentleness that is exercised with authority, even when judgment is warranted. Therefore as His ambassadors, we are called to have attitudes and actions that are worthy of that calling. In so doing, we realize the benefits of our inheritance in Him, in this life and in the life to come.

Reflection Questions

- Where in your life is God inviting you to lead with gentleness rather than force?

  ____

  ____

  ____

- How does recognizing your identity as a child of God influence how you respond to others?

Application Points

- Journal one area of your life where pride often rises—submit it to God and ask for a spirit of meekness.

- Practice listening more than speaking in your conversations this week, reflecting a posture of humility.

- Encourage someone today with gentle words, especially if they are hurting, struggling, or defensive.

Prayer Prompt

Lord Jesus, You were meek and lowly in heart, yet full of truth and power. Shape my heart to reflect Yours. Teach me to walk in humility, to trust in Your strength rather than my own, and to respond to others with patience and grace. Let Your gentleness be evident in me today, and may my life reflect the inheritance I have in You. Amen.

The Hunger of the Kingdom

"Blessed are those who hunger and thirst for righteousness, for they shall be satisfied." **Matthew 5:6**

The Anatomy of Spiritual Appetite

Have you ever known hunger, and I mean real hunger? Hunger to the point of starvation? What about thirst? Thirst to the point of gulping down gallons of water at a time? A thirst that has your throat so dry that your throat feels like sandpaper? True to form, Jesus uses imagery that takes our earthly, fleshly appetites and applies a spiritual dimension to them. In this case, He likens our natural appetite for food and drink to our spiritual appetites.

If we fill up our spirit with junk, what can you expect to experience? If we allow our minds to focus on the things of the world that corrupt our hearts and take our focus off of the heart of God, how soon do you think it will be that you find yourself wanting more of that same thing? Our appetites will dictate our actions and focus our habits. It requires a radical change in focus to shed the weight of the world.

The Weight of Worldly Consumption

For the past few years, I have struggled with obesity due to my overindulgence in food and a laziness of intent when it comes to my diet and exercise. As a result, I've taken on far too much weight and it has led to higher blood pressure, problems with my feet and knees, various aches and pains, difficulty with simple tasks like putting on my shoes. And it's not like I ballooned in weight overnight. It took a few years of disregard for my physical condition for me to realize that things had gotten out of control. But that is changing, but just as the weight didn't come on overnight, it won't go away overnight either. It will only happen through discipline and a radical change of habits.

In a lot of ways, our spiritual lives are much the same way. When we become lazy in our spiritual diets, eventually our hearts become so bloated with doubt, bitterness, anger, spitefulness, judgement, and self-centeredness. We allow people in our lives to influence our decision-making more than we allow the word of God. We allow our forms of entertainment to saturate our vision and hearing and lead our attention to desire more of the same. We find overindulge in drunkenness to the point that our lives become a blur. And it begins with incremental compromises in our hearts that turn our spiritual hunger and thirst to things that are not characteristic of righteousness.

The Call to True Satisfaction

The hunger and thirst that Jesus refers to here is a hunger to the point of starvation and a thirst to the point that your life feels dry and empty without the righteousness of God in your heart. It is a seeking after the heart of God with ever fiber of our heart, mind, soul, and body. Later in this same sermon, Jesus goes on to say "But seek first the kingdom of God and His righteousness, and all these things will be added to you." (Matthew 6:33) The emphasis and impetus is not on our own righteousness and our deeds, but on His righteousness and what He has done in our lives.

The Psalmist writes:

The Lord looks down from heaven
on the children of man,
to see if there are any who understand,
who seek after God.
They have all turned aside;

together they have become corrupt;
there is none who does good,
not even one. *Psalm 14:2-3*

And you may say to yourself, "But I am a good person. I'm better than that guy. I'm not a murderer. I'm a relatively honest person." By what standard do you comparing your righteousness? By the world's standard that shifts with the sands of time? Or by the solid rock of God's standard that is "the same yesterday, today, and forever" (Hebrews 13:8)? And if nobody is capable of achieving God's standard in this world, then how can we receive God's righteousness. The same way that Abraham received it:

Just as Abraham "believed God and it was counted to him as righteousness." Know then that it is those of faith who are the sons of Abraham. And the Scripture, foreseeing that God would justify the Gentiles by faith, preached the gospel beforehand to Abraham, saying "In you shall all nations be blessed." *Galatians 3:6-8*

God Himself, by His Spirit, imparts His righteousness upon those who hunger and thirst for Him. That is how we are satisfied. When we seek to know Him and be obedient to Him, our lives become saturated with definition and hope and peace. We experience love, joy, and grace in a new way as our hearts become broken for the things that break His. When we feed on a steady diet of His word, exercise its dictates and serve our neighbors, we shed the weight of the world and our lives become more narrowly defined. We must radically alter our spiritual habits of what we allow to consume our time and attention and intensely focus on "whatever is true, whatever is honorable, whatever is just, whatever is pure, whatever is lovely, whatever is commendable, if there is any excellence, if there is anything worthy of praise, think about these things." (Philippians 4:8)

Be hungry. Be thirsty. And fill up on the word of God. Let it change your life. Then and only then will you be truly satisfied.

Reflection Questions

- Where do I see myself in this metaphor of spiritual hunger and thirst?

  ____
  ____
  ____

- How am I feeding my soul? Am I consuming things that lead me closer to Christ or farther away?

  ____
  ____
  ____

Application Points

- Identify one worldly habit you need to "shed" this week to hunger more for God. Record it below and date it for later reflection.

  ____
  ____
  ____

- In your church or small group, create space to discuss spiritual appetites — what we feed on and how to reorient our desires toward God.

  ____
  ____
  ____

Prayer Prompt

Lord, awaken in me a hunger and thirst for Your righteousness. Forgive me for dulling my appetite with things that leave me empty. Fill me with a desire for Your truth, Your Word, and Your holiness. Shape my habits and focus my heart on You. Teach me to feast on the Bread of Life and drink deeply from the Living Water. May my soul find satisfaction only in You. Amen.

The Mercy of the Kingdom

"Blessed are the merciful, for they shall receive mercy." Matthew 5:7

Mercy and grace are two sides of the same coin. We have often defined mercy as "not receiving the judgement that we deserve" and grace as "receiving a blessing that we do not deserve." In both cases, the definition of mercy and grace imply that they are not something that is deserved or can be earned. In fact, with both, we deserve the opposite of what we receive. We tend to sum up these two words with another word that shares a similar meaning: forgiveness.

The Cost and Power of Forgiveness

But what is forgiveness? Forgiveness is perhaps one of the most misunderstood and misused words in the English language. We often say that we "forgive" someone but we continue to harbor bitterness towards the offender in our hearts. Is that really forgiveness? Does forgiveness require demonstrative, sincere confession and contrition in order to be granted? Does forgiveness imply meritorious reward for for humble repentance? Or does forgiveness inspire confession, contrition, and repentance?

If you look closely at the word, the center of the word is another word that is the root of the entire meaning of it: give. At its root forgiveness implies an act of giving of oneself to another. In fact, in the New Testament the Greek word "aphesis" that is translated as "forgiveness" is an active word that means to release as a jailer would release a prisoner. Additionally, there is a secondary definition that means "to cause to stand away". In simpler legal terms, it is the separating of a criminal from their crime, and no longer counting it against them. The offense is no longer on the record.

Let's be perfectly clear. Forgiveness does not ignore that an offense has occurred. In fact, by definition it must acknowledge that an offense exists that is worthy of punishment or restitution. However, forgiveness is absorbing the cost of the offense, choosing not to exact the just consequence from the offender. In terms of accounting, it is the act of paying for the debt owed to you out of your own funds.

Right or Reconciled?

I've often asked this question and it is rare that I get an honest, self-examined answer: "Is it more important to be right or in a right relationship?" The obvious answer would be "to be in a right relationship." But do we really believe that if we continue to harbor resentment towards someone who wronged us? Have we really mended the relationship? Or are we just easing our own conscience with false humility and buried pride? It's one thing to throw away your pride and forgive someone; it's quite another to bury your pride and shake hands while holding on and nursing a grudge waiting for the next offense to rear its head. It's the proverbial hatchet - buried with the handle sticking out ready to be surfaced to cut the offender back down to size.

Jesus put it quite simply like this: the greatest commandment is to love the Lord God with all your heart, mind, body, and spirit AND (not "BUT") the second is like it - love your neighbor as yourself. (Matthew 22:37-40) Jesus literally equated our love for God with our love for each other. If we truly love our neighbor, forgiveness should come quickly. In fact, if you are a Christ follower, knowing the price that God paid to forgive you of your sin, you forfeited all rights to have an unforgiving spirit towards anyone.

When I look upon the landscape of our country today, it breaks my heart to see a spirit of unforgiveness blanketing our land. It has manifested itself in political divisiveness and violence from every corner. What is the most disheartening is when I see self-proclaimed Christ followers DEMANDING restitution for offenses perpetrated against them. I see Christians who speak with bitterness in their words. I've seen believers go decades without speaking to one another because of simple or even complex disagreements all because they are more concerned with being right about their side of the argument than being in a right, restored relationship with one another.

Unforgiveness: The Silent Prison

Forgiveness is the most precious act of love that anyone can give. It does not require restitution because then it becomes something earned by the offender, rather than something given by the giver. Forgiveness releases the shackles of payment from the offender, but it also releases the forgiver from the chains of bitterness and resentment. Don't get me wrong - forgiveness doesn't come easy. It's not easy to let go of the hurt and the pain, especially when we have become so accustomed to it that it just seems natural and to release that pain means to venture into uncharted territory of emotional vulnerability. In its fullest context, this is the greatest blessing that extends beyond material giving and the fullest meaning of Jesus' words when He said "It is more blessed to give than to receive."

Reflection Questions

- In what ways have I confused "saying I forgive" with truly releasing someone from the offense?

  ____

  ____

  ____

- Am I more committed to being right, or being in right relationship with others — especially fellow believers?

  ____

____

____

Application Points

- Identify one relationship where you may be harboring bitterness. Ask the Lord for the courage to forgive — genuinely and fully.

  ____

  ____

  ____

- Write down what forgiveness would look like in that situation — practically and prayerfully.

  ____

  ____

  ____

- Meditate on Matthew 18:21–35 this week, and journal how the parable challenges your current view of mercy and grace.

  ____

  ____

  ____

Prayer Prompt

Lord Jesus, thank You for forgiving me at such great cost. You bore the weight of my sin, and You ask me to forgive others as I've been forgiven. Help me lay down my pride, surrender my bitterness, and walk in the freedom of forgiveness. Soften my heart, that I may love others as You have loved me. Teach me to give, even when it's hard — to release what I've held onto, and to embrace peace. In Your name, Amen.

The Purity of the Kingdom

"Blessed are the pure in heart, for they shall see God." Matthew 5:8

Purity sounds like such a insult in today's vernacular. It conjures up images of weakness, insecurity, or naivete. The Greek word ***katheros*** used in this sense means to be "clean or free of stains or corruption." That seems innocent enough on the surface, but what does it take to make something corrupted with impurities and make it pure again?

The Hidden Worth Within

Let's take a rock, but not just any rock. This rock has been underground for centuries. It has been buried under dirt, shaped by pressure and fire, molded by the shifting tectonic plates until it is metallic, with a dull sheen. Over time water erodes the stones by way of a spring that feeds into a stream or creek and pieces of these metallic stones chip away and wash downstream. Along the way, it picks up pieces of grime, dirt, other metals and types of stone. Eventually it is deposited in a stream bed along the northwestern coast of what is now known as Coloma, California.

In 1848, a man by the name of James W. Marshall, a lumber mill foreman, comes along and discovers this shiny piece of metallic rock and brings it to his boss, John Sutter. They put the rock through a series of rudimentary tests to confirm that it was indeed gold. Sutter is excited about the find, but wants to keep the discovery to himself, fearing that a rush of prospectors in the newly won California territory would upset his apple cart dreams of an agricultural empire known as New Helvetia, in what is now downtown Sacramento.

But the rumors spread and a newspaper publisher named Samuel Brannan decided to get the jump on a Gold Rush and set up a store selling prospecting supplies. After the store was set up, he then announced the discovery through the streets of San Francisco. Word reached the New York Herald in August that year and was confirmed by President James Polk. And then the race was on as prospectors from far and wide were descending upon the area hoping to make their fortunes.

But gold itself has no intrinsic value. It's nothing more than a rock. But humanity places value on gold due to what it can become. It can be shaped into fine jewelry and used to valuate currency. Its value as a commodity is dictated by the scarcity of its supply weighed against the demand for its possession. And the more pure the gold is, the more valuable it is.

The Crucible of Refinement

In order for gold to reach its highest purity, it must go through a refining process. The stones are placed under intense heat in a crucible to the point that the metallic stones melt. Once melted, the impurities and dirt and other metals rise to the top and are skimmed off and thrown away as worthless. The process is done over and over again until all of the impurities are removed from the gold and it is deemed worthy of the market price.

The same process is true of the believer. We must go through a "refining fire" to have the impurities of our heart stripped away. The blood of Christ cleanses us of those impurities, but we still have to go through a growth period where we learn how to deal with this new heart condition that we now have. A heart that is made more tender to pains of the world around us. A heart that breaks for things that break the heart of God. A heart that is sensitive to the needs of our neighbors. A heart that mourns our own sin in light of the righteousness of our Heavenly Father. Paul describes this refining like this:

"For no one can lay a foundation other than that which is laid, which is Jesus Christ. Now if anyone builds on the foundation with gold, silver, precious stones, wood, hay, straw - each one's work will become manifest, for the Day will disclose it, because it will be revealed by fire, and the fire will test what sort of work each one has done. If the work that anyone has built on the foundation survives, he will receive a reward. If anyone's work is burned up, he will suffer loss, though he himself will be saved, but only as through fire." *1 Corinthians 3:11-15*

The Master Jeweler's Work

When we turn our hearts towards our Abba, He will test us in the crucible of this life. But this testing is not to tear us down, but rather to purify our hearts and to remove the impurities and get rid of the things that stand in the way of the building of the kingdom in our hearts. His goal is to make you stronger in your faith and your dependence upon Him. It is often a painful process, but it's always a glorious and worthy process. Because in the end, our Father who earnestly demands the purest of hearts will see to it that we are purified to the highest quality.

In so doing, He declares our value. Not the world. Not your friends. Not your family. They do not do the work of refining that produces the purity in you. They do not skim off the impurities that weigh you down as much as His Spirit does. He's the Master Jeweler. He's the one who knows His craft as the Creator. He's the one who knows what and who you are intended to be. And He will shape you and mold you until you are a perfect jewel, fit for the value He holds and the price He paid to make you His.

Reflection Questions

- What "impurities" in my heart might the Lord be refining through my current trials?

  ____

  ____

  ____

- How do I view my worth — through the lens of the world, or through God's refining love?

  ____

  ____

  ____

Application Points

- Identify a trial in your life and ask God how He might be using it to purify your heart.

  ____

  ____

  ____

- Spend time in prayer this week asking the Holy Spirit to reveal hidden sins or attitudes that need refining.

  ____

  ____

  ____

- Encourage someone who is going through a difficult season by reminding them of God's refining purposes.

  ____

  ____

  ____

Prayer Prompt

Lord God, You are the Master Jeweler and the Refiner of my soul. Thank You for not leaving me as I was, but loving me enough to shape me into something beautiful for Your glory. Though the fire is painful, I trust Your hand and Your heart. Purify me, Lord, and remove all that keeps me from reflecting Your image. Make me a vessel worthy of the value You've declared over me in Christ Jesus. Amen.

The Peace of the Kingdom

"Blessed are the peacemakers, for they shall be called sons of God." *Matthew 5:9*

Are you a peacekeeper or a peacemaker? There is a massive difference between the two. A peacekeeper typically avoids conflict and works to maintain the status quo during a time of relative peace. A peacemaker is one who dives into the confrontation and seeks to bring about peace in an already divisive and contentious environment. To be a peacekeeper is more passive, while a peacemaker must take initiative and be active in the midst of strife in order to calm the storm. A peacekeeper requires relatively little energy, while a peacemaker must exert physical, emotional, and spiritual energy in order to bring about peace in the midst of conflict.

In our current state in America, you can likely classify people into three categories: peacebreakers, peacekeepers, and peacemakers. Peacebreakers are pretty easy to spot and are constantly around us stirring up strife and stoking division. One could say our national news media is a prime example of this as much of the coverage that you see on the nightly news is designed for emotional reactivity rather than thoughtful contemplation of current events. You have indoctrination from various sides of the political spectrum, but none of it is designed to build a sense of community. They speak of wanting "peace", but I fear that that is a word that they do not fully understand.

Peace that Passes Understanding

One of my favorite passages of Scripture is found in the gospel of John as Jesus says:

"Peace I leave with you; My peace I give to you; not as the world gives, do I give to you. Let not your heart be troubled, not let it be fearful." *(John 14:27)*

But what is this word "peace" that Jesus uses and what does it mean? The Greek word used is ***eirene*** which simply means "the absence or end of strife." But the word for "peacemaker" is slightly different and injects a new thought of peace as an internal state of existence. The word ***eirenopoios*** is best defined as one who makes peace in others having first received the peace of God in his own heart, not simply making peace between two parties. Now we have a clearer understanding of what Jesus meant when he said "not as the world gives, do I give to you."

From Conflict to Reconciliation

The world's version of peace is primarily external in terms of a lack of strife or conflict between two warring parties. It would say that two neighbors who settle differences over the placement of a fence yet refuse to speak to one another in the light of day were "at peace." It would say that two countries that aren't actively engaged in armed conflict are at peace, even if that peace were tenuous at best. Some would say that World War II ended with the signing of the Paris Peace Treaties in 1947. I would submit that these treaties were just the beginning of more smaller wars that have been ongoing ever since.

For over 40 years after World War II, we lived in a state of "Cold War" between the United States and the former Soviet Union which played itself out in armed conflicts in Korea and Vietnam. As Israel was established as an autonomous country, it has come under constant attack ever since because of the animosity of its surrounding neighbors towards the Jewish nation who have finally reclaimed the Promised Land of their heritage from Abraham. For over 40 years the Eastern bloc of Europe was hidden behind the Iron Curtain of the Berlin Wall, and any who tried to escape over it were often shot on sight by the guards seeking to keep them in. The ending of the World War II arguably was not the peace we hoped for even if the armed conflict had been mostly eliminated.

But the kind of peace Jesus refers to is an internal peace in the heart of each individual person, that manifests itself in loving our neighbor as ourselves. It is a peace that seeks to actively embrace one another in spite of our differences instead of avoiding one another because of our differences of opinion. It is a peace that is designed to be contagious and spread through human touch from heart to beating heart.

The Heart of a Peacemaker

It has been said that peacemakers are bridge builders spanning the chasm between opposing sides divided by a gulf of uncertainty. In order for real peace to exist between opposing parties, it must first begin in the hearts of the individuals. And more often than not, it requires another to step in and share the peace that is in their own hearts with the opposing factions. Sometimes simply offering peace into the heart of one of the two parties is enough to spread peace to all parties in the conflict.

So I must modify my earlier question just slightly and ask it again: are you a peacebreaker, a peacekeeper, or a peacemaker? If you are a peacebreaker, I pray that God's peace finds its way into your heart and that you seek to make peace with your neighbors instead of resorting to conflict, strife, or violence. If you are peacekeeper, I urge you to rethink that strategy and seek to cross the lines of division and embrace your neighbor in a spirit of real peace before the bitterness and resentment take root and build a wall around you. Eventually, as a peacekeeper you could even get caught in the crossfire of conflict between others.

However, if you are indeed a peacemaker who has found the peace of God in your own heart, then I pray that you have the strength to endure the fight to bring peace to those around you. It is often a harder battle to fight in order to breach the stone walls of a closed heart. But once you get that first chink in the armor, the rest of the wall is sure to eventually come crashing down allowing the other heart to beat anew with the same peace that lives in you.

Reflection Questions

- Am I avoiding conflict to keep peace, or am I actively pursuing reconciliation like Jesus did?

  ____
  ____
  ____

- What barriers in my own heart might hinder me from being a true peacemaker?

  ____
  ____
  ____

Application Points

- Ask God to reveal whether you are a peacebreaker, peacekeeper, or peacemaker, and commit to grow in Christlike peacemaking. Note below and date for later reflection.

  ____
  ____
  ____

- Reach out to someone with whom you've had tension and seek to understand and reconcile.

  ____
  ____
  ____

- Memorize and meditate on John 14:27 this week, praying for Christ's peace to fill your heart.

  ____

  ____

  ____

Prayer Prompt

Lord Jesus, You are the Prince of Peace. Fill my heart with Your unshakable peace, not as the world gives, but as only You can. Make me a true peacemaker—bold enough to step into conflict, yet gentle enough to heal it with love. Let Your peace overflow in me, breaking down walls and building bridges. May I reflect Your heart in every word and action, for Your glory. Amen.

The Persecution of the Kingdom

"Blessed are those who are persecuted for righteousness' sake, for theirs is the kingdom of heaven." Matthew 5:10

I firmly believe that there is a fundamental misunderstanding of what it means to be "persecuted" in the world today. While I agree that there is a concentrated effort by some to reshape the moral landscape into a more secularized image in the name of humanism and to remove the name of God from the square of public discourse, I must admit that it falls far short of a biblical definition of persecution. So much so that we have allowed the culture of victimization that we have distorted the meaning of persecution as it was described in Scripture to the point that every little thing that doesn't go our way is an example of persecution.

Discomfort or Devotion?

Yes, there are certain legal cases that are being brought to bear to try to force Christian believers to violate their Biblically informed conscience, but I wonder at times is that conscience being selectively exercised to put on a front of self-righteousness disguised as godliness. While we may experience legal difficulties, it pales in comparison to the persecution of our Biblical forefathers and others in some parts of the world today. For example, in 2015, 21 Coptic Christians were kidnapped and summarily beheaded on the beach expressly for the refusal to denounce their faith and turn to Islam. It was three years before their bodies were given a proper burial after the video-taped execution.

According to the foremost experts on global Christian persecution, Open Doors International, the United States is not even in the top 50 countries responsible for persecution of

Christians. In fact, of the top 50 countries identified for the systematic persecution of Christians, all but one (Colombia) of them are in Africa or Asia, including the Middle East.

Past and Present Martyrdom

In the Roman Empire, Nero would systematically crucify Christians and use their bodies as torches for his nightly feasts, thus giving birth to the term "Roman candle". Christian persecution in the Roman Empire reached its height, however, under the reign of Emperor Diocletian, who would summarily have Christians executed in the Circus Maximus (see picture above) on charges of treason for the crime of refusing to worship the emperor as a god.

In the United States, we still enjoy a Constitutionally protected freedom to worship our God in whatever manner we choose, even if that worship is not in accordance with Biblical truth. However, there have been efforts to restrict Christian expression in the public square. There has even been efforts by certain local governments to influence Christian doctrine from the pulpit. But it is still a far cry from imprisonment and execution.

The Greek word for persecution in this verse is "dediogmenoi heneken dikaiosunes", which is translated as "ones having been chased on account of justice". Persecution can take on many forms, but the fullest meaning is a description of "mob justice". The Jews of Jesus' day understood what this meant at the hands of their Roman oppressors who were known to systematically take over countries and annex them into the Empire. Their history is rife with examples going back to the Babylonian captivity and even Egyptian slavery prior to the Exodus of Moses. Jesus Himself would even know persecution intimately as He was tried, beaten, mocked, and crucified for daring to speak the truth and challenging the authority of the Pharisees.

Saul would persecute Christians in the early church in the book of Acts, with the full approval of the Sanhedrin and the Roman government, two levels of citizenship that he enjoyed and used to his full advantage. That is until Jesus blinded Him and knocked Him off his literal high horse, at which point he used those same advantages to spread the truth of the gospel, resulting in his own eventual beheading in Rome under the reign of Nero.

Of the twelve apostles, all but one experienced death by martyrdom. The lone survivor, John, would be boiled alive in oil, but miraculously escaped and was exiled to the island of Patmos where he lived out his remaining days after receiving his final Revelation from Christ. Fox's Book of Martyrs gives hundreds of examples of Christian leaders and early church fathers who were martyred for their faith, sometimes in gory detail. Tertullian would go on to say that "The blood of the martyrs is the seed of the church." While there are various translations of what he said, the intent of the message is clear - that the church grew because faithful believers gave their lives for the truth of the gospel.

Our Hope in the Eternal Kingdom

Martyrdom should never be a goal for our faith, but I must ask: if your life is put on the line for your faith, will it hold true? Can you honestly say that you would be willing to die for the truth of the gospel if it ever came to it? The fact of the matter, it is happening around the world today. Maybe not so much in America…yet. But don't be so naive to think that it may not eventually come. Empires rise and fall. Constitutions are rewritten. Countries live and nations die.

But our God is the same yesterday, today, and forever. He will remain faithful, even through our trials and sufferings. His kingdom is eternal, and the gates of Hell will not prevail against it. This He has promised and this He will continue to prove true, for we are citizens of His kingdom eternally.

Reflection Questions

- In what ways might I have confused cultural opposition or personal discomfort with biblical persecution?

  ____
  ____
  ____

- How can I better support and remember those around the world who are truly suffering for Christ?

  ____
  ____
  ____

Application Points

- Study the lives of Christian martyrs (e.g., through *Foxe's Book of Martyrs*) to deepen your appreciation for the cost of discipleship.

  ____
  ____
  ____

- Commit to praying weekly for persecuted believers around the world using resources like Open Doors or Voice of the Martyrs.

  ____
  ____
  ____

- Evaluate your own faith: Am I willing to stand for righteousness, even if it costs me socially or legally?

  ____
  ____
  ____

Prayer Prompt

Lord Jesus, You endured the cross for the joy set before You. Strengthen my heart to stand firm in righteousness, not seeking comfort but Your glory. Teach me to remember the persecuted and to live boldly and humbly for Your name. Make me ready to suffer well, if You call me to it, knowing that Your Kingdom is my eternal home. Amen.

Dying for the Kingdom

"Blessed are you when others revile you and persecute you and utter all kinds of evil against you falsely on my account. Rejoice and be glad, for your reward is great in heaven, for so they persecuted the prophets who were before you." Matthew 5:11-12

In the Beatitudes, Jesus speaks three times to the issue of persecution. He even hints at the possibility of an institutionalize, conspiratorial attack upon those who choose to not only live life in accordance with the dictates of God's word, but for the simple act of following Him. Of course if the religious leaders of the day, the supposed representatives of God in the Sanhedrin would go so far as to beat Him in the midst of a mockery of a midnight trial who are we to expect any less of those who would elevate themselves up to be co-equal with God Himself? Who are we to think that we are any better than Jesus, whom they falsely accused of blasphemy and insurrection against Herod for declaring Himself King?

Mind you, these are not the pagan Romans of the day (at first), but the purported believers who wielded spiritual power and authority over the people in an effort to "keep the peace" with their Roman oppressors. And to take it further, the Romans took their cues from the Jewish authorities as they held their own mockery of a trial and entertained the false accusations and in fact found Jesus "not guilty", not once, but twice in one night before Pilate casually washed his hands of the situation and released a murderous Barabbas to the raucous crowd. When they cried out to "give us Barabbas", they were literally crying out "Give us the son of the father." Granted the name "Barabbas" was a fairly common name in the first half of the first millennium, but the serendipitous irony is too much to ignore.

The first time Jesus speaks of persecution is in relation to our lives characterized by God's righteousness. The second time Jesus speaks of persecution it is in relation to our lives characterized by our acknowledgement and devotion to Him. The third time is a comparison to the prophets that went before, who were persecuted and killed by the very people they were sent to declare God's message to. The earliest mention of the killing of the prophets was when Jezebel destroyed the prophets and priests of God as she and Ahab instituted a nationalized fertility cult to Ba'al and Asherah - a religion characterized by ritualistic acts of sensuality and self-indulgence. And she wanted the prophet Elijah dead most of all.

Isaiah is said to have been sawed in two by Manasseh and buried by what is now known as the Pool of Siloam. Jeremiah died by stoning in Egypt, where he was buried and later reinterred in Alexandria (some believe that he was later re-interred again in Ireland during the Crusades). Ezekiel was martyred by the Chaldeans. Micah was martyred by King Jehoram. Amos was tortured by the priest Amaziah and the killed by one of Amaziah's sons. Jesus even mentions that the prophet Zachariah was killed by the religious leaders of his day "between the temple and the altar" by stoning. And Jesus Himself would be mocked, beaten, stripped naked, humiliated, paraded through the streets of Jerusalem, and then crucified on a Roman garbage dump outside the city.

On Resurrection Sunday, April 21, 2019, the people of Sri Lanka began their day just like any other normal day. The minority Christian population of Sri Lanka entered into worship celebrating the reality of their risen Savior. Without any warning, in a coordinated attack, 6 suicide bombers attacked 3 Christian churches and 3 prominent hotels. The attack was timed to inflict maximum devastation of Christians in worship on their holiest of days and vacationers innocently enjoying breakfast at the hotels. In all, 267 people were killed and another 500 injured.

This is what it is like to live under a regime that is hostile to the Christian faith.

And a time will come when we may endure similar attacks. We may have insults hurled against us for our faith in Christ as the only way to the Father. We may even have evil spoken against us and have false accusations levied that would even bring us into a court of law in an effort to smear our reputations, and thus the reputation of our God. While we are not currently here in America having to experience this on a institutionalized scale, it is happening already in many parts of the world that are hostile towards God. I pray that time is a long way off, but when that time comes, I pray you are prepared.

The prophets died for their devotion to the truth of God's word. Jesus died for His devotion to you. Are you willing to lay your life down for Him? "Greater love has no one than this, that someone lay down his life for his friends." (John 15:13) The Kingdom of God grows because it is watered by the blood, sweat, and tears of the true martyrs of the faith. Those who lay their lives on the line for the gospel. Those who refuse to deny the truth in the face of death. I have not faced death for my faith, and I pray I never do. I know there are times that I have failed to stand up for the gospel in the face of mere jest and ridicule. And for that I am ashamed. I pray that I am bolder and stronger today than yesterday and that I will be able to stand on the rock that is greater than I if and when that times comes.

I pray that my faith does not become centered on me, but rather stays centered on the cross of Calvary. I pray that I do not mistake discipline for persecution. I pray that I do not mistake correction for assault. I pray that God will always give me the discernment that I need that is informed by the truth of His word for whatever situation He puts me in. And I pray that I have the endurance to stand where others have fallen.

The older I get, the less I fear death and the more I fear disappointing my Abba. The words that I most desire to hear on the lips of my Lord: "Well done, my good and faithful servant." (Matthew 25:23) Anything less would be a life wasted in pursuit of less worthy goals. The only legacy worth leaving is that of being good, being faithful, and being a servant. Even if the whole world turns against me, I know that His eye will never leave me and I can always rest in the shadow of His wings.

Reflection Questions

- How does understanding the historical and present-day suffering of believers affect your view of what it means to follow Jesus?

  ____

  ____

  ____

- Are you spiritually prepared to stand firm in your faith, even if it costs you your comfort, reputation, or safety?

  ____

  ____

  ____

Application Points

- **Honor the Faithful Witness of Martyrs**: Let the stories of past and present persecution deepen your appreciation for the cost of the Gospel and strengthen your resolve to live boldly.

  ____

  ____

  ____

- **Expect Opposition**: Jesus promised persecution—not as a punishment but as a validation of faithfulness. Embrace hardship as part of the Christian journey.

  ____

____

____

- **Prepare Your Heart**: Don't wait for persecution to build your faith. Cultivate spiritual disciplines, biblical literacy, and fellowship now to prepare for future trials.

____

____

____

Prayer Prompt

Lord Jesus, You were reviled, falsely accused, and crucified for my sake. Help me to stand firm in truth and love when I am misunderstood or opposed. Strengthen my brothers and sisters around the world who suffer for Your name today. May their witness and courage inspire us to be faithful, even unto death. Amen.

The Salt of the Kingdom

"You are the salt of the earth, but if salt has lost its taste, how shall its saltiness be restored? It is no longer good for anything except to be thrown out and trampled under people's feet." *Matthew 5:13*

Salt is undoubtedly one the most common chemical compounds on the earth. It comes in many forms and in multiple chemical combinations. The most common of which is NaCl - one positively charged atomic ion of sodium and one negatively charged atomic ion of chlorine. Seawater contains an average of 2.6% salt by weight, which amounts to an estimated 78 million metric tons per cubic kilometer of water in the oceans and seas of the world.

A Timeless Treasure

Throughout the history of the world, salt has had a wide variety of applications. The most obvious use of salt is to add flavor, or rather to enhance the natural flavor of food. Prior to refrigeration it was the most common preservative of meats. In fact, the word "sausage" is derived from a word that literally means "salted meat". Our word "salad" originates from Romans using salt on leafy greens and vegetables prior to eating. It also where we get the term "salivate." If we "oversalt" our food, we ruin it. If we don't use enough salt in cooking, the food is bland and tasteless. It's all about the right amount of seasoning to perfect the dish.

It has also been used for medicinal purposes as an antiseptic. It has been used in hygiene and cosmetics as an exfoliant in soaps to scrub off dead skin cells. It is used as a bonding agent in pottery and as a chemical agent in textiles, leather tanning, fabric dyes, and bleaches. Salt is often used in dry, arid places in the world to stimulate water retention.

Salt has often been used in various religious rituals as a symbol of purity. There are numerous references to covenants in the Old Testament that were sealed with salt. The word "salvation" also comes from this element of spiritual purification.

There are also military uses for salt. The term "salting the earth" is a reference to a practice of spreading large amounts of salt on the grounds of conquered lands in order to curse the ground and prevent the growing of healthy crops. Salt is used in the production of gunpowder and dynamite.

Salt is also important to our health and diets, but in proper amounts. Too little salt in our diets can lead to blockages in the small intestines, underactive thyroid, heart failure, higher propensity for sunburn, and diarrhea. It can lead to lethargic brain activity resulting in muscle twitches, seizures, cramps, loss of consciousness, coma, and even death in extreme situations. In fact, it is reported that more of Napoleon's troops died during the retreat from Moscow in 1812 than the invasion of Moscow itself because their wounds were not properly healing due to a lack of salt in their diets.

Too much salt in our diets has been link to osteoporosis, kidney disease, and hypertension - leading to cardiovascular disease and stroke. Excessive salt in the bloods causes the body to pull more water into the bloodstream, thus increasing the volume of blood within the cardiovascular system. This puts more strain on the heart to pump the greater volume of blood, stretching the walls of blood vessels, leading to aneurysms and easy bruising.

For thousands of years, and still to this day in certain parts of the world, salt has strong economic uses beyond mere commodity as a form of currency. In fact, salt was at one time more valuable than gold due to the difficult process of extracting salt from seawater or mining from rock. The word "salary" and the phrase "worth your salt" comes from this use of salt as money.

And salt that has become damaged by misuse or neglect to the point that it has lost its usefulness cannot be made salty again. It is reduced to nothing more than a useless, grainy rock. Its purpose is then lost, which is why it is so important that salt is kept in place that it easily accessible, but secured from corruption by pests and excess water.

Extracted to be Broken

Most importantly, in order for salt to be usable, one of two processes has to happen - and in some cases - both. First, there is the process of extracting salt out of sea water. It's a difficult and time-consuming process, but it is a process that yields tremendous results. Sometimes it happens naturally as is apparent around the edges of the Dead Sea.

The other process is by mining - which requires extracting salt out of the earth and the large rocks of salt have to be broken until it is small enough to be usable by the consumer. In rare cases, even in the case of extraction of salt from seawater, this breaking process is still required to pulverize the salt into small enough grains to be of value.

Now just like gold, salt at its core is nothing more than a rock. It has no inherent value of its own beyond that which we place upon it. Today, salt is so common that it is rarely used as currency in industrialized countries. In fact, while gold does have value as a commodity for jewelry, it holds very little value as a liquid currency as even our own American dollars are no longer backed by the gold standard - but simply by supply and demand of government issued legal tender.

More Than a Valuable Commodity

When Jesus speaks of us being the "salt of the earth", He is speaking to our value. If we place our value and worth in the marketplace of the world, while over time we may see some profit, eventually we become so common that we are worthless. We lose our flavor and thus our value to society. The people of Israel know this imagery all too well as they were now an occupied people by the Roman Empire, cast aside as a backwater land with weird customs, but just valuable enough due to its location at the junction of three continents - Europe, Africa, and Asia - to retain worth to the Empire.

But in God's economy you are His most precious commodity. You are His most precious jewel. He wants to use you to bring value and flavor to the world. He wants to use you to bring healing to a hurting world and scrape out that which is dead and lifeless. He wants to use you to destroy the enemy of this world. And He wants to use you to be an agent of purification in the world.

At the same time, we must be careful not to be "too salty" to the point that we drive people away. Or not salty enough so that people are uninspired to eat more at the table of grace. We must exercise discernment to the point that we provide just enough salt for the given situation so that we sate the appetite and leave them hungering for more.

But most importantly, we must be extracted from the world, set apart, and broken so that we can be usable for the Kingdom. Our hearts must be broken for the things that break the heart of God. Otherwise, our hearts are nothing but a useless, hardened stone that beats only for ourselves.

Reflection Questions

- In what ways am I currently bringing the "flavor" of Christ into the world around me?

  ____

  ____

  ____

- Where might God be calling me to be "broken and set apart" so I can be more useful to Him?

  ____

  ____

  ____

Application Points

- Ask the Lord to search your heart and reveal areas where you may have "lost your saltiness"—your zeal, witness, or spiritual usefulness. Document any areas he brings to mind.

  ____

  ____

  ____

- Consider a specific relationship or environment (work, family, church) where you can act as a preserving and healing presence.

  ____

  ____

  ____

- Meditate on Matthew 5:13 this week and journal what it means for your identity in Christ.

  ____

  ____

  ____

Prayer Prompt

Lord Jesus, You have called me the salt of the earth—not by my merit, but by Your grace. Make me useful in Your Kingdom. Break my heart for what breaks Yours. Purify what is unclean, strengthen what is weak, and preserve my heart in holiness. May I bring flavor, healing, and hope to the world around me, always pointing others to the goodness of Your gospel. Amen.

The Light of the Kingdom

"You are the light of the world. A city set on a hill cannot be hidden. Nor do people light a lamp and put it under a basket, but on a stand, and it gives light to all in the house. In the same way, let your light shine before others, so that they may see your good works and give glory to your Father who is in heaven." *Matthew 5:14-16*

In 1990, I began my first stint with college life. As a freshman, and newly reborn believer, I invested a huge amount of time in the Baptist Student Union - now known as Baptist Collegiate Ministries. It was through this campus organization that I had numerous summer missionary opportunities in such places as Cochise County in Arizona, Hong Kong, Cuidad Acuna in Mexico, and Plaquemines Parish in Louisiana. It was also the place that I developed some of the longest lasting friendships that I still have today. One of those friendships was with a young student evangelist named Kenny Moore.

The Light of the World

I still have one of Kenny's business cards from those days. It had the usual contact information while in the background it had the picture of a lighthouse. When Kenny gave me his card, he asked if I knew what the lighthouse meant. Well, I was familiar with the old gospel song "The Lighthouse" and I assumed that it meant that the lighthouse was a representation of Jesus - a light shining in the darkness to guide us to the safety of shore. However, Kenny gently corrected my misconception when he said, "No, the lighthouse is me. It is us as believers who are called to shine the light of Jesus in the world."

Thus began my fascination with the imagery of lighthouses. I've always been drawn to paintings and photographs and posters of lighthouses. I've always loved ceramic and porcelain mantlepieces of lighthouses, even though I have none of my own to this day. And there are some things about lighthouses that I learned over the years that has stuck with me, thanks to Kenny's enlightenment.

First of all, lighthouses are not built on beaches, but rather on rocky cliffs overlooking the sea. This provides for more stability when the storms of the sea come crashing in. Secondly, a working lighthouse must never be abandoned - someone must always be there to tend to the light and ensure that it is always shining. Finally, the beacon is actually a large mirror that reflects the light within it and projecting it through a rotating lens so that it can be seen from all around.

One of the Seven Wonders of the Ancient World was the great Lighthouse of Alexandria, built during the reign of Ptolemy II, and was one of the tallest man-made structures in the world in its day. It was severely damaged by earthquakes and then abandoned to ruin. The last portions of it were used to build what is now the Citadel of Qaitbay, built in the 15th century.

In the Christian life, we are called to be a lighthouse to the world. We are called to build our lives on the solid rock of the proclamation of Jesus as the Christ, the Son of the Living God. This firm foundation is one that is unshakable, even as the storms of life come crashing in around us. The truth of Jesus as the Messiah is unchanging and eternal and is our anchor in the storm. We must anchor deep within Him and abide in Him to withstand the trials and tribulations of this life.

Secondly, we must always be tending to the light and keeping it shining. That is our number one responsibility as ambassadors of Christ - to shine the light of the King upon this dark world so that others can see the safety of shore and be warned of the dangers below. And we must always be attentive to the light, ensuring that it is shining as bright as possible so that the whole world can see Jesus for who He really is - our safe harbor in the midst of the storm.

In a typical home in Jesus' time, when it reached sundown, it was the duty of a member of the household to light an oil lamp and place it in a position so that all in the home could see in the dark. Darkness in and of itself has no substance. It's empty. When we are in the dark, it is not so much that we are "in darkness", but rather we are absent from the light. That's all darkness is - the absence of light. If you go into a dark closet and close the door, typically you can not see anything once you close the door. All it takes is the tiniest of lights - like the one on your watch - to pierce that darkness and allow a small amount of sight. The brighter the light, the greater the vision.

Finally, the light that we shine is not our own light, but it reflects His light that is focused outwards towards all around us. This is evidenced by our works of service that are done with a pure heart that seeks not its own gain or reward through pats on the back. It is so that those we minister to will come to know Jesus as the provider of eternal safety in this life and beyond. As we saw in Matthew 4:23-25, Jesus met the physical needs of those who came to Him first and then He addressed their spiritual need for the Kingdom beginning with the Sermon on the Mount.

The City on a Hill

When Jesus mentions the “city on a hill”, there was no mistaking the intended allusion to the location of Jerusalem. The capital city of Judea and home of the temple that built by Solomon, rebuilt after the return from exile, and then expanded upon by King Herod the Great to include a new area called the Court of the Gentiles, that provide the Romans access to the temple.

In ancient times, cities were generally built in one of two places. Port cities or merchant cities were built near major waterways – either on the shores of the Mediterranean Sea or major rivers. Nineveh was formerly a city built on a river, but fortified to prevent flooding with giant walls. Caesarea Maritima was a major port city on the eastern Mediterranean Sea. Capernaum was a merchant city located on the shores of the Sea of Galilee.

However, absent of direct sources of fresh water or water ways for trade, cities would then be built on high hills as a defensive measure. It would provide a vantage point for lookouts to see approaching visitors or armies. It would also provide a strategic advantage of being the high ground in the event of an attack from any would-be enemies.

Jerusalem was built on a large hill, the highest of which is Mt. Moriah, the mountain upon which Abraham was to sacrifice Isaac, but God intervened. Originally, the name of Jerusalem was simply Salem – which is loosely related to the word "shalom" and translates to "peace." When David recaptured Salem from the Jebusites, who had renamed the city to Jebus, which translates to "foundation," he made the city the capital of the nation and called in Zion, a symbolic name for God's chosen city. (2 Samuel 5:6-10) So the translation of the name of Jerusalem is literally "foundation of peace."

Solomon chose to build the temple on Mount Moriah. In so doing, the house of God was built in the most prominent location of Israel – high and visible for miles. Symbolically this also meant that God Himself had a full view of the city and its inhabitants, and was effectively a lookout for the dangers of enemies outside the city. As long as the nation was faithful to the covenant with God, they enjoyed His blessing. However, when they would abandon Him, His blessing would not be granted, for He does not bless disobedience and betrayal.

If you notice the layouts of ancient cities in Europe, there is an interesting phenomenon that you will notice. Most cities, once Christianity took hold would either be built around a local cathedral or church and as the city grew, so did the church to accommodate the rising population. Even in colonial America and well into the twentieth century, the church was the center of the local society and influenced the culture. Non-believers at least had a respect for the institution of the church as a moral beacon in society, even if they didn't bend to that ethos.

Eventually the culture "outgrew" the church and the script was flipped to the point of the culture influencing the church. As the Enlightenment took hold in Europe in the late 1600s - 1800, churches began to decline and have remained in decline ever since as postmodernism and secularism have gained a foothold. In America, in the late 20th century, beginning with the removal of Bible reading and prayer from public schools, the national moral compass has spun out of control in favor of individualistic passions. The authority of Scripture no longer holds sway in public discourse.

As a city on a hill, the Church has only one entrance and that is through submission to Jesus Christ as Lord of our lives. We are built upon a rock that is steady and sure so that the world can see that the work that we do in for the His glory, not ours. For that to be true, we must always be attentive to the light and continually submit to Him daily, taking up our cross - not a cross of obligatory burden, but a cross of victory over sin, death, and the grave. Above all, we must remember that He is the light that lives within us and we must live in a way that is reflecting His light to all around us, so that they will see the dangers below and be guided safely home to shore.

Reflection Questions

- What areas of your life are shining His light clearly—and what areas might be hidden under a "basket"?

  ____

  ____

____

How does the cultural shift away from biblical values affect your witness as a believer today?

____

____

____

Application Points

- Tend to the light daily through prayer, Scripture, and surrender to Christ, so that your life reflects His truth consistently.

  ____

  ____

  ____

- Stand firm on the Rock of Christ, even when culture shifts—your foundation determines your faithfulness.

  ____

  ____

  ____

- Live visibly as a witness. Whether in your home, community, or online, be intentional about showing Christ through works of love and truth.

  ____

  ____

  ____

Prayer Prompt

Lord Jesus, You are the true Light that gives light to every man. Thank You for calling me to reflect Your light in this dark world. Help me to build my life on the solid rock of Your Word, to tend to the flame of faith with diligence, and to live in such a way that others may see Your beauty and be drawn to

You. Keep me vigilant, humble, and bold as I shine for You. Amen.

The Law of the Kingdom

"Do not think that I have come to abolish the Law or the Prophets; I have not come to abolish them but to fulfill them. For truly, I say to you, until heaven and earth pass away, not an iota, not a dot, will pass from the Law until all is accomplished. Therefore whoever relaxes one of the least of these commandments and teaches others to do the same will be called least in the kingdom of heaven, but whoever does them and teaches them will be called great in the kingdom of heaven. For I tell you, unless your righteousness exceeds that of the scribes and Pharisees, you will never enter the kingdom of heaven." **Matthew 5:17-20**

In order for a Kingdom to exist, there must be a King. In order for a King to have any authority, there must be laws that undergird that authority. Otherwise there is chaos and anarchy, with every man for themselves. And if every person is a law unto themselves, then what happens when you have mutually exclusive, opposing moral compasses? How then would we know who is "right" and who is "wrong"? By necessity, that would require a standard that is external to ourselves in order for it to be equally applied to everyone.

Unfortunately, there are many within the Kingdom that ascribe to the idea that because we are under grace, that somehow the Old Testament law has been done away with - that somehow, the Law of Moses is no longer valid. As Jesus said Himself, He did not come to abolish or do away with the law, but rather to fulfill the law. The word here for “fulfill” literally means “to make complete”. And how does He complete the law? By becoming the very sacrifice demanded for all of the law.

The Law Still Matters

The Old Testament law required payment or sacrifice for breaking the law. There was a prescribed punishment or offering required depending on what the law was that was broken. Typically the sacrifice was of apparent equal value to that which was lost as a result of the sin. If you stole from your neighbor, then restitution would be required. This would also mean that if you commit murder or a crime of violation against another of God's image bearers, then often that would mean equal dismemberment or even death.

And Jesus said the standard of the law of Moses has not changed. His standard for our behavior is still the same. And the prescribed penalties are still in place, except with one difference. Jesus fulfilled this prescription. "For the death He died, He died to sin once for all; but the life He lives, He lives to God." (Romans 6:10) The writer of Hebrews made a clear case for Christ as the substitutionary payment for the our sin of breaking God's law in chapter 10: "First he said, "Sacrifices and offerings, burnt offerings and sin offerings you did not desire, nor were you pleased with them"—though they were offered in accordance with the law. Then he said, "Here I am, I have come to do your will." He sets aside the first to establish the second. And by that will, we have been made holy through the sacrifice of the body of Jesus Christ once for all…Then he adds: Their sins and lawless acts I will remember no more. And where these have been forgiven, sacrifice for sin is no longer necessary." (Hebrews 10:8-10, 17-18)

Grace Doesn't Cancel Obedience

Now grace and forgiveness do not mean we are given free reign to go back and continue to live a life characterized by sin and not in keeping with God's law. Nothing could be farther from the truth. This is evident even as far back as the time of the prophet Samuel:

"Has the LORD as great delight in burnt offerings and sacrifices, as in obeying the voice of the LORD? Behold, **to obey is better than sacrifice**, and to listen than the fat of rams. For rebellion is as the sin of divination, and presumption is as iniquity and idolatry. Because you have rejected the word of the LORD, He has also rejected you [Saul] from being king." (*1 Samuel 15:22-23, emphasis mine)*

Contextually speaking, Saul had disobeyed God by taking spoils from the victory over the Amalekites, specifically against God's orders. Saul then decided to take those spoils and offer them in sacrifice to God as an act of worship. Let me rephrase it like this: Saul offered the very act of disobedience as an act of worship on the altar of God. How much more blasphemous can one be? And the worst part about it is even when he was confronted with his sin, he blamed the people instead of taking responsibility for his own disobedience.

Saul said to Samuel, "I have sinned, for I have transgressed the commandment of the LORD and your words, because I feared the people and obeyed their voice." *1 Samuel 15:24*

Well, you might say, "I would never do such a thing." But do we not? Do we harbor grudges against our brother/sister as we enter into worship? Have you ever wished harm to someone in the name of "justice" for the sake of our own self-righteousness? Do you judge the appearance of the person sitting in the pew next to you, or decide instead to sit on the other side of the sanctuary to avoid them? Do you sit in worship and ignore the sermon in favor of following your social media feed? Have I relegated my tithe to the end of my budget, giving God only a portion of what remains, instead of the first fruits of my harvest? Do you give your offerings expecting a blessing from Him in return, as opposed to expecting to be a blessing for the

Kingdom? Have we ever done an actual honest assessment of our heart in the midst of our ritualism?

Righteousness or Ritualism?

It's not the sacrifice that God desires, even though the law prescribes it. It's obedience. He desires our obedience to His word. But not obedience out of blind obligation. Not obedience out of ritualistic incantation. To do so reduces the name of Jesus to an act of witchcraft - which is blasphemy of the highest order.

Jesus wants our heart. He wants our devotion. We obey His word because we know that He loves us and He proved His love for us by taking the punishment that we deserve. That doesn't mean that we escape consequences for our sin that we commit today, even though we are forgiven. Consequences are still inevitable.

The very idea that there is a moral concept of "right" and "wrong" is evidence of a natural, moral law that we are all bound to. If there is a natural or moral law, then by common reason there is a moral law giver. A law giver who has given us a guide by which we as His people are called to obey.

And Jesus challenges us in our obedience. Our righteousness must "exceed that of the scribes and Pharisees." These scribes and Pharisees were keepers of the law. They knew the letter of the law down to the smallest mark. And they followed it to the letter, but did not hide the spirit of the law within their hearts. They followed the law out of a spirit of ritualistic obligation rather than heartfelt devotion to the God who delivered Israel from the bondage of slavery to Egypt. But God desires our devotion - that we follow the law out of reverence and humility, as opposed to vanity and pride. Then and only then will our righteousness exceed that of the scribes and Pharisees for it will be a righteousness that is imparted to us by Him through the Blood of Christ due to our faith in His word.

Reflection Questions

- In what ways might I be offering outward religious acts to God while withholding my obedience?

____

____

____

- Do I seek to obey God's Word from a place of love and devotion, or from obligation and fear?

____

____

____

Application Points

- Examine your heart for areas of disobedience masked by religious routine. Ask God to reveal anything you've withheld from His lordship.

____

____

____

- Renew your understanding of the Law as a reflection of God's holiness and Christ's character. Seek to obey not to earn grace but because grace has been given.

____

____

____

Prayer Prompt

Lord Jesus, thank You for fulfilling the Law on my behalf. Teach me to love Your commands and to obey them with a whole heart. Create in me a clean heart and renew a right spirit within me. May my worship be more than words—may it be obedience born out of love. Amen.

The Heart of the Kingdom

"You have heard that it was said to those of old, "You shall not murder; and whoever murders will be liable to judgment." But I say to you that everyone who is angry with his brother will be liable to judgment; whoever insults his brother will be liable to the council; and whoever says, "You fool!" will be liable to the hell of fire. So if you are offering your gift at the altar and there remember that your brother has something against you, leave your gift there before the altar and go. First be reconciled to your brother, and then come and offer your gift. Come to terms quickly with your accuser while you are going with him to court, lest your accuser hand you over to the judge, and the judge to the guard, and you be put in prison. Truly, I say to you, you will never get out until you have paid the last penny." Matthew 5:21-26

The heart of the gospel of the Kingdom is the atoning death and resurrection of Christ for the forgiveness of sins that produces a heart for reconciliation. Anger that drives a wedge between people to the point of spiritual division within the body of Christ breaks the heart of God. The act of murder is an act born of hatred and unreconciled anger. And by the letter of the law, murder required judgement that exacts the price of death. But Jesus takes the letter of the law further and gets to the heart of the law. If unreconciled anger is at the root of the act of murder, then the heart of the matter is that anger makes one just as guilty as the one who commits the act.

Anger and the Heart of the Law

Now let me be perfectly clear. Biblically speaking, anger in and of itself is not a sin. Paul writes in Ephesians 4:26-27: "Be angry, and do not sin; do not let the sun go down on your anger, and give no opportunity to the devil." By definition, anger is nothing more than an emotional response to unmet expectations. The question comes down to the righteousness of our expectations. Jesus Himself showed anger at various times within His ministry, but His anger was justified. In every case of anger that Jesus displayed, it was the case of where religious authority was abused to the point of twisting God's word to manipulate His children. And nothing throughout the history of the Old Testament or the New Testament burns the wrath of God more than those who intentionally lead God's people astray. That is why some of the harshest penalties of the law of Moses were reserved for false prophets. (See Deuteronomy 13:1-5)

There are plenty of things to be legitimately angry about in this world. Human trafficking. The selling of children within the sex trade. Racism. Murder. All of these are crimes against the image bearers of God himself. And it's particularly heinous when such crimes are perpetrated against innocent children. These are things that anger the heart of God and should anger all of us. However, the heart of the gospel is one that seeks to reconcile sinners to grace of God. Yes, even the murderer. Yes, even the racist. Yes, even the seller of children and other human traffickers. And there are nothing in this world that burns my own heart to anger more than the scourge of child sex trafficking. However, the truth of the matter is that it is the only the grace of God that brings repentance, not the other way around. The only way we end human trafficking is to reach the heart of traffickers and inspire repentance. The only way we reach end racism is to transform the heart of the racist with the gospel of Christ that reconciles all people until Him.

And Jesus speaks directly to the heart of the gospel by getting to the heart of the law within the heart of mankind. If you have anger in your heart to the point of hatred for another person, then yes, you are just as guilty as if you had murdered them. While there may not be legal consequences, there are surely spiritual consequences that impact your soul. Whether it be an individual or a class/group of individuals. When we look at the cross of Calvary, and recognize the price God paid to reconcile us, we are called to surrender our unforgiving spirit in view of the cross. And when we harbor anger, bitterness, and resentment within our hearts, we shackle the gospel and put it in a box reserved for those that we find deserving of grace. The truth of the matter is that none of us deserve grace. Otherwise, it isn't grace; it's merit. If God can forgive an adulterous, murderous, liar of a king to the point that he is restored and called a "man after God's own heart," then He can change the heart of anyone that is willing to seek transformation. Anyone.

The Call to Reconciliation

And I speak from experience. There have been different people in my life that I have harbored anger and bitterness towards over the years. And every time the name of that person would come up, it would make my heart twist and my head grow cold. And the reality of it all is that my anger was borne out of my own self-righteousness in those cases. My prideful need to be right. In many of those cases, I have sought reconciliation and forgiveness for my attitude towards those individuals. In other cases, I am still working on that. Forgiving and seeking forgiveness.

Now forgiveness and reconciliation do not always mean that the relationship will go back to "normal". It doesn't mean that you will be best friends with one another. But it does mean that you no longer hold the offenses of one another to account. The debt is cleared. The line item is vetoed. In fact, by definition, the heart of the word "forgiveness" is "give." It means you give grace and take the debt that is owed upon yourself. That is what Jesus did on Calvary. That is what we must do with one another for the sake of the Kingdom.

Unresolved anger, bitterness, and unforgiveness within the body of Christ makes a mockery of the cross of Christ. Yes, we are called to hold one another accountable to the law of God and the heart of God. And we must remember that anger does have a proper place and should inspire us to hold one another accountable in a spirit of love. However, the goal of such discipline is not separation, but reconciliation. Discipline is intended to spur repentance in the heart of the offender and reconciliation between parties, but ultimately full reconciliation in our mutual relationship to our Abba Father.

Reflection Questions

- Is there unresolved anger in your heart that Christ is calling you to surrender?

  ____

  ____

  ____

- How does the cross shape the way you view those who have deeply wronged you—or those who are hardest to forgive?

  ____

  ____

  ____

Application Points

- Ask God to reveal any anger, bitterness, or resentment hiding in your heart. Confess it and take the first step toward reconciliation where possible.

____

____

____

- Commit to viewing others through the lens of the cross—not through their worst actions or your deepest hurts.

  ____

  ____

  ____

- Pray for the ability to forgive, even when reconciliation in relationship may not be fully possible. Grace begins with giving.

  ____

  ____

  ____

Prayer Prompt

Father, You forgave me when I was Your enemy. You gave grace when I deserved wrath. Help me reflect Your mercy by surrendering my anger and bitterness. Teach me to forgive as You have forgiven me. Soften my heart, Lord, and reconcile me to those I've held at a distance. Let my life reflect the peace of the gospel. In Jesus' name, Amen.

The Passion of the Kingdom

"You have heard that it was said, "You shall not commit adultery." But I say to you that everyone who looks at a woman with lustful intent has already committed adultery with her in his heart. If your right eye causes you to sin, tear it out and throw it away. For it is better that you lose one of your members than that your whole body be thrown into hell. And if your right hand causes you to sin, cut it off and throw it away. For it is better that you lose one of your members than that your whole body go into hell." **Matthew 5:27-30**

Our basest human desire is the desire for love. It is the desire for relationship and attention from someone who genuinely cares about our best interests. This is followed very closely by our desire to love another. But all too often, when we don't feel love, we default to lust. And this leads to more problems than you can possibly imagine in the world.

The Corruption of Love

At its root, lust can be defined as the selfish objectification of someone or something that is not rightfully yours. And this extends beyond mere sexual lust, but into the realm of covetousness as well. A lust for power. A lust for sex. The lust for life. These are mere examples, but they demonstrate the animalistic, objectifying nature of our default human existence as a result of sin. And in our society, we tend to excuse and rationalize this sin more than any other because it appeals to our basic human appetite for affection and attention.

Lust is not simply restricted to the male gender; women are susceptible to lust as well. For men, however, it is more visual because God designed men to be hunters. Women, on the other hand, tend more towards emotion and the need for security.

Now before you get all offended and accuse me of chauvinism and not being "woke" enough, I'm not saying the women are weaker than men and require the security of a man in order to have value. Men and women are both uniquely created and designed by God to complement one another, not to compete with one another. As such, because we are created by God in His image, we ought also to treat one another and look upon one another as such, rather than see each other for what we can gain from them.

The primary difference between love and lust is this: lust seeks to take another unto oneself, whereas love seeks to give of oneself to another. In the English language we have just one word for love, and it takes on a variety of meanings depending on the context. In Greek, there are four different words for love, each with its own contextual meaning: 1. storge – familial love, 2. phileo – brotherly love or friendship, 3. eros – erotic love, 4. agape – sacrificial love.

For a long time, our society and even the church has treated eros as an evil kind of love, or at the very least, a lesser form of love. God designed sexual attraction for the purpose of recreation between a husband and wife and procreation as a natural product of that love. The sexual act is designed to be a picture of the intimacy of the spiritual unity that God desires with His creation. However, our sinful nature has perverted this gift and we have allowed it to destroy humankind on so many levels.

In the United States alone, the sexual exploitation that defines the pornography industry generates over $12 billion annually – more than the combined annual revenues of the big three broadcast networks ABC, CBS, and NBC. That's an average of over $3000 every minute. It is estimated that between 20 and 40 million people around the world are trapped in modern slavery, with more than 80% of those in sex trafficking, which profits roughly $150 billion a year, with nearly $100 billion of it from commercial sexual exploitation. The average age of a person entering the sex trade in the United States is between 12 and 14 years old. Globally an estimated 71% of all enslaved people are women and girls, with 98% of them in the sex trade. And if you think that men are the only perpetrators of sexual exploitation and partaking of this trade, you'd be sorely mistaken; it is estimated that closer to 25% of such perpetrators are women, and that number is climbing annually. (See footnotes for citations.)

God's Vision of Human Dignity

So if you think lust is a "victimless" sin or at worst "self-harm," you'd be very wrong. Lust belittles the personhood of one of God's image bearers to the level of an object to be desired, used, and abused, rather than sees them as a person to be loved. It reduces men and women to the level of nothing more than a product of animalistic passions rather than people of inherent, created value.

And God's passion is for the benefit of His creation. His passion is to see you as a person of worth. His desire is for us all to see one another as He sees us. And He wants us to be passionately aware of our value to Him. When we start to see one another as a person of worth that God created with value, that changes the way we treat them. If we want to see an end to human trafficking, we must find a way to change the heart of traffickers and the hearts of buyers. There must be a transformation of the heart so that we do not see human sexuality as a commodity to be traded on the market, but rather as a gift to be given within the confines of Biblical marriage between a man and a woman, as God designed us to complement one another.

What You Feed, Grows

As believers, we must be careful of what we expose ourselves to in our entertainment. I need to be careful of some of the more "innocuous" programs that I expose myself to as well. The books that I read. The music that I listen to. The art that I purvey. Are these forms of entertainment glorifying God? Am I allowing the window of my soul to be open so far to allow the pollution of the world to corrupt my heart? Are you? I urge you, please be discerning of what you willingly allow yourself to partake in. If the lyrics of the song objectifies another person, turn it off. If the books you read, celebrate the immorality of our world, put it away. If the art you peruse treats displays another human being in a manner that is unfitting of their God given value, walk away. If the program you are watching objectifies men or women, turn it off.

I'm not saying it's easy. I'm not saying we are all going to be immediately aware that what we are viewing is not what we should be. But if we start to see our fellow humans, man and woman alike, the way that God sees us – as people of value worthy of love, respect, and dignity, then it will start to come more naturally. I'm not perfect, but I'm getting better. And I still have a long way to go. And by the grace of God, I will get there.

Statistical Footnotes:
https://enough.org/stats_porn_industry_archives
https://www.dosomething.org/us/facts/11-facts-about-human-trafficking

Reflection Questions

- In what ways have I allowed the world's view of love and sexuality to shape my thoughts more than God's truth?

  ____

  ____

  ____

- Do I truly see others—as well as myself—as image-bearers of God, worthy of dignity, not exploitation?

  ____

____

____

Application Points

- Evaluate the media, music, and entertainment you consume. Does it honor God and respect His image in others?

  ____

  ____

  ____

- Replace lustful desires with Spirit-led actions that build love and serve others selflessly (Gal. 5:16–24).

  ____

  ____

  ____

- Commit to seeing others through the lens of God's design, valuing their worth beyond their physical appearance.

  ____

  ____

Prayer Prompt

Lord, purify my heart and renew my mind. Teach me to see others as You see them—worthy of love, respect, and dignity. Help me flee from lust and live in the freedom of Your love. Give me eyes to see the image of God in every person and courage to walk in holiness. Amen.

The Covenant of the Kingdom

"It was also said, "Whoever divorces his wife, let him give her a certificate of divorce." But I say to you that everyone who divorces his wife, except on the ground of sexual immorality, makes her commit adultery, and whoever marries a divorced woman commits adultery." Matthew 5:31-32

Marriage is not a legal contract. Marriage - Biblical marriage - is a covenant between one man, one woman, and one Triune God. Marriage, from the beginning, was always designed to be a picture of the intimate relationship that God desires between His creation and Himself. In the beginning, God took a rib from Adam, and created Eve. Adam's response was "This is bone of my bone, and flesh of my flesh." These words iterated the unity and covenant nature of marriage.

Cleaved Together

Several years ago, I conducted a demonstration before a church audience that illustrated this covenant unity. I stood before the congregation, and I poured super glue onto my hands and then placed them together. This was to demonstrate the joining together of man and wife in the bonds of matrimony and the intimacy that unity is designed to inspire.

However, I also explained that because my hands were now fused together, if I were to rip them apart, pieces of the palms of my hands and fingers would end up ripping off and remain stuck to one another. Yes, the hands would be separated, but the separation would be intensely painful and those torn pieces would forever be stuck on each hand. That is unless I used some acetone or fingernail polish remover to dissolve the glue.

The Threat of Divorce

This is the picture of what happens spiritually and emotionally to two people who go through a divorce. Divorce is ugly. It's messy. It's painful. And for years, people who have gone through divorce will carry the baggage of that torn relationship with them. It will impact future relationships in ways that are difficult to predict.

"For I hate divorce," says the Lord, the God of Israel, "and him who covers his garment with violence," says the Lord of hosts. "So take heed to your spirit, that you do not deal treacherously." (Malachi 2:16)

God Himself through the prophet Malachi equates divorce with an act of violence against one another. The reason for God's hatred of divorce is simple: the marriage covenant was always intended to reflect the relationship between God and His creation. As two people who are created in His image are joined together in covenant marriage, it is a picture of God's desire to be joined eternally with His creation. It's no wonder that Paul uses the imagery of marriage to describe the church as the Bride of Christ (cf. Ephesians 5:25-32). He desires you individually as His bride, as well as the whole of the ekklesia.

I use the term "covenant" to reference marriage because it's something much deeper than a mere legal contract. A covenant in Scripture, within the Old Testament, is initiated between two parties and then is sealed with a blood oath or sacrifice. The blood oath or sacrifice is intended to be offered by both parties as a statement that essentially means "May it be done to me what is done here if I should ever break this covenant." You can see this on display in Genesis 15:7-21 when God makes a covenant with Abraham.

Now the breaking of a covenant is serious business. In many cases, the breaking of a covenant would even lead to war. In Biblical marriage, this same principle applies. A bride and groom come together and they make covenant vows to one another, forsaking all others, until death do they part. But in a divorce, the couple inflicts spiritual and emotional violence upon one another. This is why God clearly states that He hates divorce.

If you have been through a divorce, there is grace enough for you at the foot of the cross of Jesus. The blood of Christ is sufficient to cleanse you of the stain of divorce. The grace of Christ is sufficient to make you new again.

If you have not experienced divorce, I urge you do whatever is necessary to avoid it. While divorce is indeed forgivable, the consequences of divorce are still far reaching and will linger with you for years to come. It will surface in ways you can't possibly predict. It will magnify your insecurities and even embolden your arrogance if not dealt with. Repentance doesn't necessarily mean reconciliation, although I can recall many different cases of couples who have divorced and then remarried again after reconciling, and with much counseling.

If you have not yet been married, I encourage you to not be frightened by the statistics. Nearly 60% of all marriages today end in divorce. The statistics within the church - sadly - aren't any better. In fact, in the 1990s divorce among professing Christians surpassed that of the culture, and hasn't looked back. But you do not have to be another statistic. Go into your relationship with your eyes opened. Honor one another and treat each other with the respect and dignity that is becoming of God's creation. And when you find your "one", I would encourage you to go through pre-marital counseling to make sure you are both aware of what awaits you beyond the wedding altar. A wedding is just a ritual ceremony, but it is a sacred ceremony that demonstrates the unity of man and woman before God. But a wedding is not a marriage. A wedding can take months to prepare and execute, a marriage takes a lifetime.

Reflection Questions

- How does viewing marriage as a covenant before God—not just a legal arrangement—change the way I approach relationships?

  ____

  ____

  ____

- How does seeing marriage as a reflection of God's desired relationship with you change your perspective of your daily habits?

  ____

  ____

  ____

Application Points

- If you are married, take intentional steps to nurture your relationship through prayer, mutual respect, and accountability. Don't wait for problems to arise—invest now.

  ____

  ____

  ____

- If you are single/engaged, pursue pre-marital counseling and develop a Christ-centered view of marriage that honors God from the start.

  ____

  ____

  ____

- In the same way, take intentional steps to nurture your relationship with God through prayer, daily Bible study, and frequent fellowship with your local Christian church. Invest in your Kingdom relationship now.

____

____

____

Prayer Prompt

Father, thank You for the gift of marriage and the picture it paints of Christ and the Church. Help me to honor the covenant You designed, whether in marriage, singleness, or past wounds. For those who are hurting from broken vows, I ask for healing and grace. For those walking faithfully in marriage, I ask for strength and humility. And for those preparing for the future, I ask for wisdom and discernment. Let all our relationships reflect Your glory and point to the redemptive love of Jesus. Help me to see my relationship with you as a covenant relationship sealed by your blood for all eternity so that I might pursue you with the same fervor as I would a life partner. Amen.

The Oath of the Kingdom

"Again, you have heard that the ancients were told, 'You shall not make false vows, but shall fulfill your vows to the Lord.' But I say to you, make no oath at all, either by heaven, for it is the throne of God, or by the earth, for it is the footstool of His feet, or by Jerusalem, for it is the city of the great King. Nor shall you make an oath by your head, for you cannot make one hair white or black. But let your statement be, 'Yes, yes' or 'No, no'; anything beyond these is of evil."
Matthew 5:33-37

I've heard it said through the years that if you have to preface a statement with "I promise..." or "To be honest...", odds are you aren't. We use phrases like "I swear on a stack of Bibles" or "On my ancestor's grave...". In fact, I once started to say "Well, if I'm being perfectly honest..." and was interrupted with "Well, why start now?"

It used to be that a person's word was their bond, that you could take a person at their word without hesitation, because a person's reputation rests upon their ability to keep their word without the necessity of extra persuasiveness. Unfortunately, that does not appear to be the case so much in the world today.

A Biblical Oath

In Old Testament times, a covenant was often sealed with an oath and a sacrifice. The oath or pledge was a declaration of the responsibilities of both parties in the covenant. The sacrificial element of the covenant was representative of the punishment that would befall whoever would break the covenant. In today's vernacular, this is similar to legal covenants in which there is a financial penalty imparted to the person that breaks the covenant.

To break a vow was the equivalent to breaking the commandment to not lie or bear false witness. To swear an oath by Heaven or by Earth is to suppose that Heaven or Earth are yours to sacrifice in the event of the breaking of the oath. In reality, Heaven is the throne of God and Earth is His footstool. While these are metaphors, the meaning to the listeners of the Sermon on the Mount and to Matthew's audience is clear - you cannot offer up sacrifice that is acceptable that doesn't belong to you - that would have no impact upon you directly if you break the covenant. Put simply, Jesus is telling us when you say you are going to do something, do it without the necessity of extra reassurances. Let your actions fulfill your words.

Taking the Lord's Name

We can take this a step further when you consider the full contextual meaning of Exodus 20:7: "You shall not take the name of the Lord your God in vain, for the Lord will not leave him unpunished who takes His name in vain." In light of this context as the third of the commandments of God, this statement is in fact a declaration of the seriousness of the covenant that God was making with His people. God had just declared in verses 5-6 that He will not only visit the iniquity of the fathers on the children to the third and fourth generations of those who hate Him, but He will show mercy and kindness to those who love Him and keep His commandments.

To seal this covenant as part of the tribe of Israel was to "take the name of the Lord your God." To take His name in vain was an attempt to have all the benefits of the covenant (mercy) without the responsibilities of the covenant (obedience). The term "vain" is best described as "empty" or "meaningless". This is the root word for "vanity" that is used throughout Solomon's words in Ecclesiastes to describe the emptiness and worthlessness of life under the sun, compared to the riches and glory of God Himself. The second part of Exodus 20:7 makes it clear that God will not withhold the covenant prescribed punishment from those who do not keep their word to the covenant - a covenant that demands repentance.

A Covenant Walk

Now, let's be very clear here. Eternal salvation is granted by the grace and favor of God Himself, not a result of our obedience itself. This is clearly explained by Paul in Ephesians 2:8-9 when he writes "For by grace you have been saved through faith; and that not of yourselves, it is the gift of God; not as a result of works, so that no one may boast." But Paul doesn't discount the value of obedience as he continues in verse 10 with "For we are His workmanship, created in Christ Jesus for good works, which God prepared beforehand so that we would walk in them."

Our works of obedience are still important and are a demonstration of our repentance that is inspired by God's grace. When we come to Christ and become a "fisher of men", we make a public declaration of this covenant through the sacrament of baptism. If you have not truly surrendered your heart to the covenant relationship with God through Jesus, then your baptism was nothing more than you getting wet. Baptism does nothing mystical, it is simply a symbolic gesture of taking of the oath to follow Christ in your daily life.

If you say that you are a Christ follower, then let your life show it. Live the dictates of God's Word. Learn the responsibilities of the covenant that you have sworn to uphold. You can trust God at His word because He has proven Himself true time and again throughout history. If you truly examine yourself, can you honestly say that God can take you at your word?

Reflection Questions

- When I give my word, do others see the integrity of Christ in my life?

  ____

  ____

  ____

- Have I taken the name of the Lord in vain by claiming to follow Him without living in obedience?

  ____

  ____

  ____

Application Points

- Study God's Word to understand the responsibilities of the covenant you have entered through Christ.
- Let your daily communication be so honest that others never need additional assurances or oaths.
- Let your baptism reflect a heart that has truly surrendered to Christ—not just a public ritual, but a personal transformation.

Prayer Prompt

Lord, You are a faithful covenant-keeping God. Teach me to walk in integrity, to speak with truth, and to bear Your name with reverence. Thank You for the grace that saves and the Spirit who empowers me to live out that grace. Help me to be a person whose yes is yes, and whose life reflects the truth of Your Word. In Jesus' name, Amen.

The Grace of the Kingdom

"You have heard that it was said, 'An eye for an eye, and a tooth for a tooth.' But I say to you, do not resist an evil person; but whoever slaps you on your right cheek, turn the other to him also. If anyone wants to sue you and take your shirt, let him have your coat also. Whoever forces you to go one mile, go with him two. Give to him who asks of you, and do not turn away from him who wants to borrow from you." **Matthew 5:38-42**

There are endless stories of the transformative power of grace, but do we really and truly understand what grace is and how powerful it really is to transform a life? I've often stated that grace can be defined as "giving a gift which is undeserved." This is to contrast the definition of mercy as "not giving the punishment that which is deserved." In both cases, there is inherently the implication that what we deserve is far worse than what we receive. The offense or sin is not excused; in fact, it must be acknowledged for grace or mercy to have its maximum impact. However, we must understand the origin of grace—God Himself—is what makes it so transformative. In both cases, it is a deliberate act of the will to love in spite of the circumstances that warrant anger and judgement.

The Law of Grace

When Jesus quotes a common saying of the day "An eye for an eye, and a tooth for a tooth" he's is not quoting the Old Testament law. He's quoting a common tradition that originated with the Code of Hammurabi, who was king of Babylon from 1792-1750 BC. It was a law among the Babylonians over 1200 years before the Babylonian exile, and even predated the Exodus by another approximately 500 years. However, it was the basis of a system of justice that the Jewish law implemented in terms of the principle of letting the severity of the punishment equal the severity of the crime. It is a principle we know today as equal restitution. It was a practice of law arbitrated by the courts, but had devolved into a form of vigilantism, where victims or their families would take it upon themselves to execute judgement outside of the courts. Herein lies the danger of allowing law that was not dictated by God to infiltrate a society, because then we see a shift from the righteousness of the Kingdom to the righteousness of the individual who has been offended.

What Jesus is talking about here is to resist the temptation to take matters into your own hand and act out of a spirit of vengeance and self-righteousness. Furthermore, He takes it a step further and commands that we actively give grace to our attacker. If an evil person slaps you, our natural inclination is to strike back. If a vindictive person wants to take your clothes off your back in court, our natural inclination is resisting and not give them anything. If they force you to go a mile, go further than what is demanded. And if anyone wants to borrow from you, don't reject them. In all these cases, the implication is that the first person listed is undeserving of the second person's commanded response. And in each case, Jesus commands us to act individually with a heart of grace.

Let's be clear here. Jesus is not speaking to the religious authorities of the day, nor is He speaking to the state authority. He is not dismissing the importance of societal order, nor is He suggesting that criminals should go unpunished in society. What He is saying, however, is to not be consumed by hatred and anger and react to injustice with emotional reactivity. Furthermore, He does go further and says we ought to as individuals extend grace to our offender in the hopes that it would change their hearts.

In 2020 - 2021, we saw a rise in violent mob justice in response to the injustice of the case of the murder of George Floyd. In fact, there have been multiple occasions over the last several decades of rioting and looting in response to societal injustice. While I completely understand the natural sentiment of those that choose to react in this manner, this is the antithesis of what Jesus is calling us to be as the Church. It is what makes the Bride of Christ different from the society in which we live. It is a message that all too often, many Church leaders choose to ignore in favor of stoking the flames of violence against the state as a form of "civil disobedience" in spite of the fact that it is the very opposite of what Jesus commands us to do and who He commands us to be.

The Transformative Power of Grace

One of my favorite stories of all time was the story of a criminal vagabond who spent an inordinate amount of time in prison for stealing a loaf of bread to appease the hunger of his widowed sister's seven children. After 20 years in prison, he is branded a criminal for life and must carry papers that bear the mark of his crime for the remainder of his life, thus effectively extending his imprisonment for the remainder of his days. This act of un-grace hardens the heart of this man and he spends his life scrounging from town to town. At one point, he even steals a coin from a child. See how far un-grace can twist the heart of a man.

Eventually, the criminal is found sleeping in an alley by a servant who offers him shelter with in the home of a priest. The priest offers him a warm meal and a bed to sleep in for the evening. He even offers him a place to stay for a time, and work to pay his own way. The criminal scoffs and in the middle of the night, he steals all of the silverware from a cupboard and as he is making his way out of the home, the priest happens upon him and the criminal assaults him.

The next day, the priest answers a knock on his door and it is the police with the criminal as he had been caught. Still nursing the wound on his head, he listened as the police officer recounts how the criminal had said the priest had gifted him the silverware. The priest, stands looks the criminal dead in the eye, and says "Yes, I did. But you forgot the most valuable pieces - these two silver candlesticks." The criminal stands astonished, knowing that he doesn't deserve this act of grace that the priest has bestowed upon him. Before the police leave, the priest looks at the criminal and utters these words:

"Forget not, never forget that you have promised me to use this silver to become an honest man. Jean Valjean, my brother: you belong no longer to evil, but to good. It is your soul that I am buying for you. I withdraw it from dark thoughts and from the spirit of perdition, and I give it to God!"

Of course, from here you must know the story of how Jean Valjean would go on to become an honest man, building a business in a small town, caring for a local prostitute named Fantine, and upon her death, adopting her child Cosette. Throughout the remainder of the novel, Valjean is hounded by the specter of his past. Inspector Javert - representing a spirit of unforgiveness and the effects that it has on Valjean's life is contrasted with the life changing grace of the Bishop Myriel. In the end of the novel, as Jean Valjean lays dying, the candlesticks are lit and rest upon the table at his bedside. He dies beneath their glow, basking in the sweet illumination of grace that has come to change his life and gifted him the blessings of fatherhood and ultimately peace.

Victor Hugo's novel Les Misérables, is widely considered one of the greatest masterpieces, if not the definitive masterpiece of French literature. It is the story of the transformative power of grace to triumph over the hardened heart of un-grace. It is a timeless story that still resonates today through history and art. Most importantly it is a story that speaks to heart of the gospel. In Victor Hugo's own words:

"The book which the reader has before him at this moment is, from one end to the other, in its entirety and details … a progress from evil to good, from injustice to justice, from falsehood to truth, from night to day, from appetite to conscience, from corruption to life; from bestiality to duty, from hell to heaven, from nothingness to God. The starting point: matter, destination: the soul. The hydra at the beginning, the angel at the end."[1]

1. *Alexander Welsh, "Opening and Closing Les Misérables", in Harold Bloom, ed., Victor Hugo: Modern Critical Views (NY: Chelsea House, 1988), 155; Vol. 5, Book 1, Chapter 20*

Reflection Questions

- When have I found it hardest to extend grace? What held me back?

  ____

  ____

  ____

- How does Jesus' teaching in Matthew 5 reshape my response to personal injustice?

  ____

  ____

  ____

Application Points

- **Extend Grace Deliberately**: Practice giving undeserved kindness in your daily interactions—especially when you feel wronged.

- **Resist Reactive Justice**: Commit to leaving vengeance to God and pursuing righteousness in your own heart (Rom. 12:19).
- **Embrace Redemptive Opportunities**: When confronted with someone's sin or brokenness, look for ways to reflect Christ's mercy and truth.

Prayer Prompt

Lord Jesus, You showed me grace when I least deserved it. Help me to remember that I belong no longer to evil, but to good—because of Your sacrifice. Teach me to extend grace as You did, not in my strength, but by the power of Your Spirit. Let my life reflect the light of those candlesticks—the light of Your redeeming love. Amen.

The Love of the Kingdom

"You have heard that it was said, "You shall love your neighbor and hate your enemy." But I say to you, love your enemies and pray for those who persecute you, so that you may be sons of your Father who is in heaven; for He causes His sun to rise on the evil and the good, and sends rain on the righteous and the unrighteous. For if you love those who love you, what reward do you have? Do not even the tax collectors do the same? If you greet only your brothers, what more are you doing than others? Do not even the Gentiles do the same? Therefore you are to be perfect, as your heavenly Father is perfect." Matthew 5:43-45

Jesus has already mentioned that hatred towards your brother is the equivalent of murder borne in the heart. However, here He revisits hatred and moves from hatred towards someone with whom you are bound to in a covenant relationship (within the body of Christ) to someone that is outside of that intimate relationship. In fact, He says that we ought to not only love our neighbor but to also love those who actively seek to destroy us.

Love Your Enemies

For the fourth time, Jesus shifts the topic of His message to contrast the heart of the Mosaic law to the traditional practice found in non-Scriptural sources. "You shall love your neighbor and hate your enemy." The Kingdom law of the Moses dictated that you shall "Love your neighbor as yourself." Period. There is no additional commentary beyond this. In fact, Jesus said in another episode "The second [greatest commandment] is [like] this: 'Love your neighbor as yourself.' There is no other commandment greater than these." The first greatest commandment of course is "You shall love the Lord your God with all your heart (kardias - affection) and with all your soul (psuche - life force) and with all your mind (dianoia - will) and with all your strength (ischus - physical strength)." (Mark 12:31, Greek commentary mine)

In fact, the transitional phrase "The second is [like] this…" is can literally be translated as "In the same manner, the second greatest commandment is…". In other words, just as we are commanded to love God with every bit of the essence of our being - our emotional affections, our life, our will, and our physical capacity - we are commanded to love other people. Jesus makes no distinction here between friend or foe. He makes no distinction between brother, sister, or stranger. Put simply, the entirely of the law is summed up in four words "Love God. Love people." Anything less than these two simple statements is sin.

Love the Hostile

Now in the Sermon on the Mount, Jesus does address the nature of two different types of relationship. He addressed the nature of hatred towards a brother / sister - someone with whom you have an intimate relationship, but harbor resentment and unwarranted anger towards. Then He takes it a step further and commands that we love our enemies - those who actively seek to harm and abuse us. Those who seek to take advantage of us. Those who seek to spitefully use us for their own selfish gain.

Furthermore, He contrasts the difference between those who would follow His teaching with those who are not His followers: "For if you love those who love you, what reward do you have? Do not even the tax collectors do the same? If you greet only your brothers, what more are you doing than others? Do not even the Gentiles do the same?" The tax collectors of Jesus' day were despised as traitors because they were often Jewish citizens who submitted to the authority of Rome and were often known to take advantage of the taxpayers. It's easy to greet those that are your friends, but far more difficult to greet those that are your enemies and make them feel at home. Even the cultural outsiders love those that love them. Emotional love is easy, because it's reflexive; but love that transcends emotion often requires a difficult act of the will.

Release from Prison

Consider the case of Corrie ten Boom. She and her family were arrested by the Nazis during World War II for hiding Jews in a secret room carved into the wall of her own bedroom. She and her sister Betsy were sent to Ravensbrück prison camp - or more literally, a death camp. Together, they would endure the hardship of the harsh treatment of their Nazi captors and even the jeering and mocking of their fellow prisoners. More importantly, despite their circumstances, and much to Corrie's own consternation, Betsy would choose to love her fellow captors in spite of their mockery. The last thing that Betsy would tell Corrie before she would succumb to typhus were two simple words: "Don't hate."

Corrie would take these words and they would go on to transform her life. In the midst of her mourning, she would encourage her fellow prisoners until one night her name was called out. Shaking in fear, believing that she was on her way to die, she bravely declared the gospel of love to her fellow captors. She gave her smuggled Bible to one of her fellow prisoners and encouraged her to cling to it. Within a few hours, Corrie was on her way home - released due to an apparent "clerical error", when all women prisoners her age were sent to the gas chambers just 2 weeks later.

Until her dying day, Corrie would travel the world teaching about the grace and love of God and teaching us all to love our enemies. She even had an opportunity to put this teaching into practice as one of her tormentors approached her after one of her teachings and declared their newfound faith and begged her forgiveness for her treatment in Ravensbrück. Corrie, pushing back the tears and anger and bitterness, extended her hand in grace and love towards this former prison guard, recognizing that they themselves had been a prisoner of their own guilt and released them to the freedom of grace.

Corrie's mission in life was to deliver a very simple message, delivered to her by her dying sister Betsy: "There is no pit so deep that God's love isn't deeper still."[1] No matter how dark your world may be, or how strong your enemy comes against you, God is capable of giving you the strength to love them and set them free from the chains that bind their hearts. Unforgiveness is a relentless prison. Grace is the key that unlocks the prison doors. Grace transforms the heart in ways that set us apart from the world. Grace makes all the difference.

1. Corrie ten Boom, Elizabeth Sherrill, John Sherrill (1971). *The Hiding Place*. Guideposts Associates. ISBN 0-912376-01-5.

Reflection Questions

- How does Jesus' command to love our enemies confront your natural instincts?

  ____

  ____

  ____

- In what ways have you seen or experienced enemy love as a testimony to the gospel?

  ____

  ____

  ____

Application Points

- Ask God to reveal any hidden resentment or hatred in your heart and repent of it (Psalm 139:23–24).

____

____

____

- Pray for someone who has hurt you, and seek a tangible way to bless them (Matthew 5:44).

  ____

  ____

  ____

- Meditate on Christ's love for you while you were still a sinner (Romans 5:8) and let that fuel your love for others.

  ____

  ____

  ____

Prayer Prompt

Lord Jesus, You loved me while I was still Your enemy. Fill my heart with that same radical love, that I may bless those who curse me and forgive those who hurt me. Teach me to reflect Your mercy, not just to my friends, but especially to those who oppose me. Amen.

The Discretion of the Kingdom

"Beware of practicing your righteousness before men to be noticed by them; otherwise you have no reward with your Father who is in heaven. So when you give to the poor, do not sound a trumpet before you, as the hypocrites do in the synagogues and in the streets, so that they may be honored by men. Truly I say to you, they have their reward in full. But when you give to the poor, do not let your left hand know what your right hand is doing, so that your giving will be in secret; and your Father who sees what is done in secret will reward you." Matthew 6:1-4

One troubling trend in today's social media culture is the increasing need to announce and dramatize acts of service and "good deeds." While good works are undeniably important—being part of God's calling—they lose their spiritual impact when the focus shifts from glorifying God to glorifying self. Acts that were meant to direct attention to the Lord instead become spotlights for personal recognition, diminishing their intended purpose.

Some argue that sharing such acts online is meant to inspire others. While that intention is understandable, the nature of social media often distorts the message. The spotlight typically lands on the individual performing the deed rather than on God. Anyone can perform kind actions, but the deeper question remains: to what end, and whose glory is being sought?

Is service done to ease a guilty conscience, or is it truly motivated by a desire to meet others' needs and point them to the Father as the ultimate provider? Is there a need to "sound the trumpet" when stepping into service, or is the goal to serve quietly, without seeking recognition or praise? Do churches highlight their service efforts as a way to attract donors and new visitors, or do they simply seek to honor Christ in their obedience?

Performative Righteousness

Jesus warned against public displays of charity intended to earn the approval of others. In His day, it was common for religious leaders to make shallow shows of generosity while their hearts were far from God. He discouraged such "performative rightesousness" because they robbed these acts of their spiritual power. Those who serve to be seen will receive the attention of men - but that will be their only reward. In contrast, sharing what God is doing in His Kingdom shifts the focus back to where it belongs: on Him.

The difference between self-promotion and God-glorifying testimony is often clear. Does the message emphasize the individual, their actions, sacrifices, and efforts? Or does it lift up what God has done - what it cost Him to reconcile humanity, how He provides, and what His purposes are in the world? Is the spotlight on the servant, or on the Savior? Is more time spent talking about personal sacrifice than about the grace of Jesus Christ?

Dr. Henry Blackaby once said in *Experiencing God*, "Do not ask God to bless your work. Rather, find out where He is working and join Him there, for it is already blessed." God doesn't call His people to forge their own path. He calls them to join Him in His Kingdom work. Human plans and programs are often shaped by limited perspective, personal ambition, and weakness. But God's work is always pure, always purposeful, and always designed for growth and the advancement of His glory.

The apostle Paul regularly encouraged believers in their acts of service, yet always pointed back to the work of God rather than the efforts of man:

"I thank my God in all my remembrance of you, always offering prayer with joy in my every prayer for you all, in view of your participation in the gospel from the first day until now. For I am confident of this very thing, that He who began a good work in you will perfect it until the day of Christ Jesus." (Philippians 1:3–6)

"For we are His workmanship, created in Christ Jesus for good works, which God prepared beforehand so that we would walk in them." (Ephesians 2:10)

Keep your eyes fixed on the King and His work. Let the spotlight fall on the only One worthy of all praise and glory. Human righteousness fades quickly under the brilliance of His holiness. Only His grace has the power to cleanse, to restore, and to truly shine. And that is the light most worth sharing.

Reflection Questions

- In what ways might my service—whether public or private—be drawing attention to myself rather than to Christ?

  ____
  ____
  ____

- How can I better discern where God is at work and humbly join Him in that mission?

  ____
  ____
  ____

Application Points

- Before serving, prayerfully consider whether the act is being done for God's glory or for personal recognition (cf. Col. 3:23–24).
- Look for opportunities to serve that are unseen by others, modeling Jesus' call to humility in Matthew 6:1–4.
- When sharing stories of ministry, emphasize what God has done, not what was accomplished personally.

Prayer Prompt

Father, search my heart and purify my motives. Teach me to serve in secret, not for the applause of men, but for Your glory alone. Help me to find joy in lifting up the name of Jesus and to join You in the work You are already doing. May my service reflect Your grace and point others to the Savior. Amen.

The Prayer of the Kingdom

"When you pray, you are not to be like the hypocrites; for they love to stand and pray in the synagogues and on the street corners so that they may be seen by men. Truly I say to you, they have their reward in full. But you, when you pray, go into your inner room, close your door and pray to your Father who is in secret, and your Father who sees what is done in secret will reward you. And when you are praying, do not use meaningless repetition as the Gentiles do, for they suppose that they will be heard for their many words. So do not be like them; for your Father knows what you need before you ask Him." Matthew 6:5-8

Prayer is not a tool for the proud, but rather it is a petition of the weak. If you spend more time in prayer glorifying yourself and your deeds and your own personal value to the kingdom, then you have completely missed the point. Prayer is about humbly submitting ourselves before our Sovereign, yet merciful God, recognizing that we do not have all the answers, but He does. By His providence, He sees our past, our failures, our mistakes, and our sin. By His grace, He forgives knowing that His Son paid the penalty for our transgressions. By His omniscience, He knows what our future holds before we even imagine it.

A Posture of Pious Pride

In Jesus' day, it was a common practice among the religious elites to not only walk around with bells on the hems of their robes to announce their coming, but at certain times of day they would suddenly and without provocation stop and loudly pray in the street - bringing attention to themselves. In many cases, contextually speaking, these prayers would be spiked with pride and self-aggrandizement. Other times, they would point out the sins of others or give thanks for their high position relative to others around them.

Jesus illustrated this with the parable of the Pharisee and the Tax Collector, which is related by the gospel writer Luke. Two men enter the temple to pray, one a Pharisee (the religious elite) and one a despised tax collector. And Jesus made a point to describe the tax collector as "despised." It was more of an indictment of the heart of the Pharisee than the condition of the tax collector. Tax collectors were often locals who would volunteer to collect taxes on behalf of Rome in exchange for protection or relief from their Roman oppressors and were often paid out of the taxes they collected - resulting in some cases over taxation for the benefit of the collector.

The Pharisee's prayer was full of selfish pride: "I thank you, God, that I am not like other people—cheaters, sinners, adulterers. I'm certainly not like that tax collector! I fast twice a week, and I give you a tenth of my income." (Luke 18:11-12) Oh the hubris! The pride. The arrogance to stand before a holy God and compare yourself to another of His creations, when the only comparison that should be made is to Him alone. When we stand in the darkness of our sin, we are blinded to our own wretchedness in comparison to Him. However, when we stand in the light of His holiness, we stand exposed for all that we truly are.

The Posture of a Prayerful Heart

And the tax collector in Jesus' parable knows this all too well. His own prayer is a simple confession: "O God, be merciful to me, for I am a sinner." (Luke 18:13) And acknowledge not only of His own spiritual condition, as is our own condition before a holy God, but a plea for mercy. It is a shorter version of Isaiah's prayer before the throne of God:

"Woe is me, for I am ruined! because I am a man of unclean lips, and I live among a people of unclean lips; for my eyes have seen the King, the Lord of hosts." *Isaiah 6:5*

Genuine prayer sheds light upon the holiness of God and exposes our nature by this same light. When we see God for who He truly is, we see ourselves for who we really are. And it changes us. For better or for worse, it transforms us. Either we fall on our face in repentance before Him, or we run away rejecting His authority. Often times, this rejection will play itself out as we live lives contrary to His word. We demonstrate a rejection of His authority by our own refusal to repent of our own selfish agendas.

Consider the words of your prayers. If the focus of your petitions before God shines more light on you than it shines on Him, then I beg you to re-examine your heart. I beg you look upon God for who He truly and deservedly is. Contemplate His holiness. Meditate upon His mercy. Embrace His grace. Then and only then will your prayers prevail upon the ears of righteousness and move the heart of our Abba.

Reflection Questions

- When you pray, do you find yourself seeking God’s presence or validating your own performance?

  ____

  ____

  ____

- How does a deeper awareness of God's holiness affect the way you approach Him in prayer?

  ____

  ____

  ____

Application Points

- Review recent prayers and ask, "Was I seeking God's glory or my own?"

  ____

  ____

  ____

- Begin prayer by acknowledging your sinfulness and your need for God's mercy.

  ____

  ____

  ____

- Focus your heart daily on His holiness, grace, and sovereign rule — let these truths shape your petitions.

  ____

  ____

  ____

Prayer Prompt

Heavenly Father, I come not with pride or performance, but with a heart that longs to know You. Strip away the self-righteousness in me and reveal Your holiness that I might see my true condition and fall before You in humble repentance. Let my prayers lift high Your name and not my own, for only in You is mercy found, and in Christ alone is grace given. Teach me to pray as one forgiven, not as one deserving. In Jesus' name, amen.

The Petition of the Kingdom

"And when you are praying, do not use meaningless repetition as the Gentiles do, for they suppose that they will be heard for their many words. So do not be like them; for your Father knows what you need before you ask Him.

Pray, then, in this way:
'Our Father who is in heaven,
Hallowed be Your name.
Your kingdom come.
Your will be done,
On earth as it is in heaven.
Give us this day our daily bread.
And forgive us our debts, as we also have forgiven our debtors.
And do not lead us into temptation, but deliver us from evil.
For Yours is the kingdom and the power and the glory forever.
Amen.''' Matthew 6:9-13

Have you ever had someone repeatedly making the same demands of you to the point that suddenly feel like you are trapped in a scene of Groundhog Day? A common practice among the pagan Romans of the day was to repeat the same ritualistic phrases over and over again in a form of magical incantation, meant to manipulate the gods into doing the will of the pray-er. Subtly, the Jewish leadership began to model this same practice by repeating the Scriptural prayers of old so much so that they began to lose the heart of their prayers and turned prayer into another form of incantation in order to manipulate God into doing their will. In fact, there are some elements within the modern church today that still practice this concept, and have taken the Lord's prayer and turned it into this same ritualistic practice, instead of recognizing the context of what Jesus was saying in order to inspire the people to approach prayer as a time of intimate conversation with their Creator.

Relational over Ritual

When Jesus says "Pray, then, in this way", He was not saying to only pray with these words. Rather, the phrase "in this way" is more appropriately translated "in this pattern." There have been a number of different acronyms and illustrations of how to pattern your prayers after the model that Jesus presented here. However, here are some highlights that will guide you through how prayer touches the heart of God.

First, we begin with the intimate acknowledgement of our relationship to Him. He is our Abba. Our intimate Father. The head of our household. The Father who guides, teaches, and disciplines because of His great love for His children. And even though He may not be physically present with us, His spiritual presence is always with us.

For many, the idea of viewing God as "father" carries some painful implication due to the relationship (or lack thereof) with an earthly father. The idea of "father" either conjures up images of abuse, neglect, or abandonment. This is an image that our Heavenly father never intended for you to endure for While no earthly father is perfect, He is the perfect Father that disciplines instead of abuses, nurtures instead of neglects, and comforts instead of abandons. Only He can be for you what no earthly Father could ever be.

Secondly, the acknowledgement of our relationship to Him inevitably inspires an acknowledgement of His holiness. When we humbly approach the throne of grace, recognizing He is the only Holy and righteous God, we are forced to recognize that we are wretched in comparison to His surpassing greatness. He is the King of Glory and we must be dependent upon His mercy.

Beholden to the Kingdom

Which brings us to His Kingdom. He is not only our Father, He is also our King. He is our lawgiver and we are citizens of His kingdom, adopted into His family and naturalized into His realm. As such we are now beholden to His word and submitted to His Lordship in our lives. As a result our priority is to shift to His will in our lives, not our own.

Next we transition to our petition for our daily need. Our manna, the bread of heaven. That which gives us nourishment and strength for the challenges of the day. As Jeremiah lamented over the pending destruction of Israel, he uttered the familiar encouragement:

"The Lord's lovingkindness [mercies] indeed never cease, for His compassions never fail.
They are new every morning; Great is Your faithfulness." (Lamentations 3:22-23)

Confessional Repentance

From here, as we bask in the glory of His grace and mercy, we are then inspired to confession. As the apostle John wrote "If we say we have no sin, we are deceiving ourselves and the truth is not in us. If we confess our sins, He is faithful and righteous to forgive us our sins and cleanse us from all unrighteousness. If we say that we have not sinned, we make Him a liar and His word is not in us." (1 John 1:8-10) John writes these words not to the unbelievers of his day, but to the church - the believers who claim the name of God. When we walk in the Light of His truth, we can quickly see that we are indeed sinners in need of mercy. And when we confess our sinful nature and our specific sinful acts, He is faithful to forgive and righteous in His cleansing. Only the righteousness of God can cleanse our own unrighteousness by the power of the Blood of His Son.

This transitions us into repentance. A heart that is forgiven is one that seeks to remain in the mercies of God. And this requires continual repentance and submission of our sinful will to the righteous will of God. It's not enough to confess our sin and depend upon His mercy. If our confession does not result in repentance, it is a faithless confession and our words ring hollow when presented from a heart of stone.

Ultimately, our prayers must be reflective and submitted to the will of God. For the Kingdom is His. The power is His. The glory is His. None of it belongs to us. We have no right to make demands of our God, but He joyfully wishes to bless His children who are submitted to the will of His Kingdom.

The great mystery of grace is not that we can approach the throne of the King and bring our demands, but rather that we can "approach the throne of grace with confidence, so that we may receive mercy and find grace to help in time of need." (Hebrews 4:16) We can approach His throne confident in knowing that when we come before Him with humility and brokenness of heart, He is faithful to place His hand upon our head and heart and give us His full approval.

Reflection Questions

- When you pray, are you more focused on God's presence or your own requests? Why do you think that is?

  ____

  ____

  ____

- How does viewing God as both Father and King shape the way you approach Him in prayer?

  ____

  ____

  ____

Application Points

- Pray through the Lord's Prayer slowly this week, using each phrase as a springboard for personal conversation with God.

  ____

  ____

  ____

- Write out a prayer of confession and repentance, focusing on God's mercy and grace.

  ____

  ____

  ____

- Take time to adore God for His holiness before bringing your requests to Him.

  ____

  ____

  ____

Prayer Prompt

Heavenly Father, You are holy, sovereign, and full of mercy. Thank You for inviting me into Your presence through Jesus. Help me to pray not with empty repetition but with a heart full of reverence, trust, and love. Shape my prayers to reflect Your will and not my own. Lead me into deeper communion with You. In Jesus' name, Amen.

Fasting for the Kingdom

"Whenever you fast, do not put on a gloomy face as the hypocrites do, for they neglect their appearance so that they will be noticed by men when they are fasting. Truly I say to you, they have their reward in full. But you, when you fast, anoint your head and wash your face so that your fasting will not be noticed by men, but by your Father who is in secret; and your Father who sees what is done in secret will reward you." **Matthew 6:16-18**

The modern Jesus that we have become so accustomed to stands in stark contrast to the true Jesus of Scripture. We cling to the passages of Scripture that expound upon His miracles and lift up those that demonstrate His grace and mercy. Yet we temper the strong words of judgement and warning and often skip over those passages that make us look at ourselves in a manner that requires repentance of our behavior. And today's passage is no different.

Reflective Perceptions

Fasting is a spiritual discipline that is purposed for our spiritual and our physical health. When we fast for our physical health it is to allow our bodies time to expel the waste and toxins that weigh our bodies down. When we fast for our spiritual health, it is to expel from our hearts the attitudes and behaviors that weigh our spirits down. But if we do so in a spirit of self-centeredness, seeking to draw attention to ourselves - we've completely missed the point.

I will be honest and admit that fasting is not a discipline that I have taken seriously within my personal spiritual walk. Unfortunately, it shows as I have a personal weakness for food. For years I have lacked discipline in the kinds of food that I eat, choosing foods that are high in sugar, highly processed, cheap, and often - delivered. It has been a symptom of gluttony and slothfulness. As a result, over the years I have allowed my body to expand from the 150 lbs. I weighed when I graduated high school 35 years ago to where I was "more than twice the man" I used to be. While I am currently on the downward trend of weight loss, I will never get back down to what I was in this picture, nor should I want to be that grossly underweight. But it is going to take intention, discipline, and determination to get the body that God has given me to steward into a condition where He can use me more effectively in this world.

The same attitude of gluttony and slothfulness can also play out in our spiritual lives as we actively gorge on entertainment and activities that distract us from the spiritual disciplines of obedience to God's word. We also passively and lazily waltz through our Christian life without being intentional about our spiritual diets, content to have our spiritual experience delivered to us instead of getting up and doing the work that God calls us to do.

Performance vs. Transformation

And when we fast, be forewarned. Don't find yourselves going around complaining about how fasting makes you feel, drawing attention to yourself. In the days of Jesus, it wasn't that uncommon for those who were fasting to take the practice for granted and just go through the motions, but neglect their personal hygiene so that others might see how "spiritual" or "holy" they were. In fact, there were many examples of different monastic figures who would take different vows to deny themselves of some earthly pleasure in order to show the world how set apart they were, often at the expense of their own health, leading to their own personal demise. Even the modern practice of Lent has taken on a watered-down, pseudo-ritualistic meaning as parishioners take a 40 day vow to abstain from some menial, often non-sacrificial pleasure like chocolate or coffee, yet still enjoy their drunken Saturday nights and feasting. As a result, the hypocrisy of the practice undercuts the heart of the discipline.

And Jesus wants against such an attitude of self-aggrandizement. If the purpose of your fasting is to simply say, "Hey look at me! I'm taking part in this ritual.", then you've completely missed the point. When we draw attention to ourselves by participating in a discipline that in intended to draw our attention to the Father, we short circuit the power and intent of that discipline.

But when you are intentional about your spiritual practice and focus your attention on the Father and His will, His favor will rest upon you. His authority will be imparted unto you. His grace will be imputed to you. His strength will sustain you. And His vision will transform your vision within your heart.

Reflection Questions

- In what ways have I turned spiritual disciplines into self-serving rituals?

  ____

  ____

  ____

- What behaviors, attitudes, or appetites do I need to "expel" through biblical fasting?

  ____

  ____

  ____

Application Points

- Before beginning any fast, ask yourself whether your focus is on God or on gaining attention from others.

- Identify areas of physical or spiritual gluttony and sloth, and seek God's transforming grace.
- Plan a season of focused fasting, pairing it with Scripture meditation and prayer, asking God to align your desires with His.

Prayer Prompt

Father, forgive me for the times I've turned spiritual disciplines into self-serving displays. Cleanse my heart of pride and complacency. Help me to fast with humility and joy, drawing closer to You in spirit and in truth. Restore my hunger—not for the things of this world—but for righteousness, for Your Word, and for Your presence. In Jesus' name, Amen.

The Treasure of the Kingdom

"Do not store up for yourselves treasures on earth, where moth and rust destroys, and where thieves break in and steal. But store up for yourselves treasures in heaven, where neither moth nor rust destroy, and where thieves do not break in and steal, for where your treasure is, there your heart is also." Matthew 6:19-21

What is your most prized possession? What do you value more than anything in this world? For many years, for me, it was my baseball card collection. While it did not hold much monetary value, there were certain cards in my collection that had the potential to explode in value in the distant future. Rookie cards for such great childhood heroes like Craig Biggio, Mike Scott, and Ken Griffey, Jr. Late career cards for other heroes like Nolan Ryan, Randy Johnson, Tom Seaver, Cal Ripken, Jr., Bobby Bonilla, and many others. And cards for the notorious Mark McGwire, Jose Canseco, Sammy Sosa, Barry Bonds, Pete Rose, Roger Clemens, and more.

Fleeting Value

The value of these cards would fluctuate over time, but in most cases they would only rise - perhaps pennies per year. Cards that were printed with errors often would fetch a higher price. Some of my favorite rookie cards, however, would take a huge hit when Jose Canseco published his shocking expose "Juiced", where he admitted to using steroids his entire career. Then the BALCO steroid scandal of 2005 broke out, tarnishing the careers of such All-Stars as Alex Rodriguez, Rafael Palmeiro, McGwire, and Sosa. All of these were in my prized collection as I grew up playing the grand old game and their value diminished overnight. Ultimately most of them were lost in

2011 when we moved from Alaska back to Texas. I still have a handful tucked away in a small binder, but their value to me has been reduced to mere sentimental value.

Scandal and corruption destroys value. They destroy reputation. But the root of scandal and corruption comes down to the desire to lift yourself higher than you ought to be by artificial means. The desire to be greater than you rightfully are. The treasure of fame and fortune is elevated over integrity and honor. Ultimately, such treasure is fleeting, for it is simply temporary. As long as you keep yourself on top of your game, and don't get caught cheating, the fame remains.

As Billy Joel once put it:

"I am the entertainer
The idol of my age
I make all kinds of money
When I go on the stage
Ah, you've seen me in the papers
I've been in the magazines
But if I go cold I won't get sold
I'll get put in the back in the discount rack
Like another can of beans."
The Entertainer, by Billy Joel, (c) 1974

Vessel of Value

One of the great commodities of the Biblical period was olive oil. In fact, olive oil, due its difficult extraction process and wide use for cooking, bathing, lamp fuel, and many other uses, it quickly replaced salt on the top of the commodities trade in the Roman Empire. Olive oil was often shipped in large clay jars call amphoras, that would have two round handles on the top for carrying. These amphorae were also highly fragile as earthenware and would easily break if not handled with care. A testament to their fragile nature can be seen at Monte Testaccio, an artificial hill in Rome made up of broken shards of amphorae pottery, measuring 115 ft high and a little over half a mile around the base. It is widely believed to be the largest garbage dump in the ancient world, measuring over 220,000 square feet with a volume of over 580,000 cubic meters, containing the remains of an estimated 53 million amphorae. A short distance away is the east bank of the River Tiber, where the Roman government would store their olive oil reserves in the late 2nd century AD.

At one time, the Pope used to use the hill to commemorate Good Friday remembrances, representing the hill of Golgotha in Jerusalem where Jesus was crucified. The Pope would lead a procession up the hill and place crosses there to represent Jesus and the two thieves that were crucified there. To this day, there is still a cross on top of that garbage heap.

During the 1st century AD, a major shipping port and exporter of olive oil was the settlement of Corinth. And Paul alluded to the value of this commodity when we wrote to the Corinthian church:

For God, who said, “Light shall shine out of darkness,” is the One who has shone in our hearts to give the Light of the knowledge of the glory of God in the face of Christ. But we have this treasure in earthen vessels, so that the surpassing greatness of the power will be of God and not from ourselves; we are afflicted in every way, but not crushed; perplexed, but not despairing; persecuted, but not forsaken; struck down, but not destroyed; always carrying about in the body the dying of Jesus, so that the life of Jesus also may be manifested in our body. For we who live are constantly being delivered over to death for Jesus’ sake, so that the life of Jesus also may be manifested in our mortal flesh. So death works in us, but life in you. 2 Corinthians 4:6-12

Investing Eternally

So I ask you again, what do you treasure most? Is it the material wealth of this world? Or is it the surpassing glory of God that overcomes the world? Is it the shekels of men or the shekinah glory of the Father? Where do you invest your time and talents? Do you spend your time on worthless and empty pursuits or do you invest in others and building up the Kingdom of God "on earth as it is in Heaven"? Are you more invested in seeking Warhol's "fifteen minutes of fame" or seeking the honor and approval of eternity?

When my time comes, and I pray that it is still decades from now, the only thing that will matter is what I have built for the Kingdom of God. Everything else will pass away. The corruption of this world will ultimately destroy the wealth of this world. That which is valuable today will lose its value tomorrow. Placing your faith in the corruptible will ultimately corrupt your faith. But placing your faith in the incorruptible glory of Almighty God will withstand the passage of time and beyond into eternity. It will define your legacy more than any bank account or measure of passing fame will.

Reflection Questions

- What are the “earthly treasures” in your life that you may be tempted to value too highly?

  ____

  ____

  ____

- In what ways can you begin storing up treasure in heaven starting today?

  ____

  ____

  ____

Application Points

- Evaluate your priorities this week by looking at how you spend your time, money, and attention. Are they directed toward eternal things?

  ____

  ____

  ____

- Invest in people and the Kingdom. Find one practical way to encourage, disciple, or serve someone this week.

  ____

  ____

  ____

- Guard your heart against pride. Pray for humility and a renewed desire to exalt Christ over self.

  ____

  ____

  ____

Prayer Prompt

Lord, help me to treasure what You treasure. Teach me to store up eternal riches and to see through the emptiness of fleeting fame and fortune. Fill me with the light of Christ, and let that light shine through my fragile life to reveal Your glory. Make me a vessel of honor, and help me invest in the things that truly last. Amen.

The Vision of the Kingdom

"The eye is the lamp of the body; so then if your eye is clear, your whole body will be full of light. But if your eye is bad, your whole body will be full of darkness. If then the light that is in you is darkness, how great is the darkness!" Matthew 6:22-23

For nearly a decade, I worked for a tech company in Austin, TX that bills itself as a "digital experience platform" and our CEO is a woman who has led the company through some tremendous challenges over the last few years. One statement that she uses quite often is "Where there is focus, there is progress." And this maxim has played itself out as we have experienced tremendous growth in our company and industry over the last 4+ years that I have been with the company. Part of this concentration on focus has been to strategize around the challenges that face us as a company. Often that strategy requires a shift in focus as we make data driven decisions about what our customers need in order to enhance their experience on our platform.

Focus Breeds Progress

Focus drives vision. But if you have no vision of what you wish to accomplish in life, you will flounder and be left wondering why others are passing you by. If business leaders do not have a vision of where they want to take their company, it is impossible to build an effective strategy to get there. The same principle applies to the spiritual life of believers, except that our vision ought to be the vision that God has planted in our hearts to advance His kingdom.

Proverbs 29:18 says it best: "Where there is no vision, the people are unrestrained, but happy is he who keeps the law." It is interesting that the writer of this proverb equates vision with obedience. And where we focus our attention will determine the degree of our obedience. If you invest your time and energy in worthless pursuits that do nothing to further the reach of God's Kingdom, then you are effectively not living in obedience to the calling for what God expects of us as His children.

If you were to take an honest inventory of the daily activities of your life, what would that tell you about where your focus lies. Do you spend hours vegetating in front of your streaming screens or do you invest time sitting at the feet of Jesus studying God's Word? Do you spend time carousing the local party scene or do you invest time in discipling other believers? Do you hide yourself away in the cave of your isolation or do you reach out to touch the lives of others with the grace that God has given to transform your heart? Do you pollute your mind with worthless wanderings or are you transformed by the renewing of your mind with the wonder that comes from gazing upon the glory of God? Does your vision extend no further than the hand in front of your face or do you have a vision the extends to the uttermost ends of the world?

Truth be told, I am very afraid of what such an inventory would say about my own investment in God's vision for His kingdom. Am I doing enough to shine light upon the glory that is His kingdom? Am I investing enough time in His word? Am I allowing my eyes to follow after the glitz and glitter of shekels of men? Am I allowing my pride to dictate that my rights are more important that His mandates? Do I treat His measureless grace as a license to sin believing that it is better to seek forgiveness than to ask permission?

Visionary Ambassador

Citizenship in the Kingdom of God doesn't come with individual rights; it comes with the privilege to confidently approach the throne of grace and the responsibility and duty to serve our King. When we come to Christ and kneel at the foot of the cross of Calvary, we lay down our rights to ourselves and take on the responsibility of being an ambassador for the Kingdom. Often we will find our vision clouded by our sin and blurred by our self-interests. It is then that we need the corrective lens of the Word of God to see clearly His vision for His Kingdom.

When we focus our eyes upon His word and start to read it not for what we can get out of it, but rather study it to get to know Him so that we can answer the question "Who is the King of Glory, the LORD strong and mighty, the Lord mighty in battle." (Psalm 24:8) We must learn to "Lift up your heads, O gates, and lift them up, O ancient doors, that the King of glory may come in." (Psalm 24:9) We must open our eyes to who He truly is and let Him into our daily hearts and lives. Then and only then can we truly and honestly declare "Who is this King of glory? The LORD of hosts, He is the King of glory."

Reflection Questions

- What does the way you spend your time each day reveal about the true focus of your heart?

  ____

  ____

  ____

- In what ways might your personal rights or desires be clouding your vision of God's Kingdom?

  ____

  ____

  ____

Application Points

- Take a weekly vision inventory. Examine how your time, thoughts, and resources are being spent. Are they aligned with Kingdom priorities?
- Refocus through the Word. Commit to reading Scripture not only for personal benefit but to better know and obey the King.
- Live as an Ambassador. Daily remind yourself that you represent Christ to the world, and seek opportunities to reflect His grace and truth.

Prayer Prompt

Lord Jesus, You are the King of glory, strong and mighty. Open my eyes to see Your vision for my life. Help me to set aside distractions, surrender my self-centered rights, and focus my heart on serving Your Kingdom with joy and obedience. Let Your Word be the lens through which I see my purpose, and may I reflect Your glory wherever You send me. Amen.

The Master of the Kingdom

"No one can serve two masters; for either he will hate the one and love the other, or he will be devoted to one and despise the other. You cannot serve God and wealth." Matthew 6:24

Who your master is will be evident by what drives your vision. Either wealth is a tool, or it will make you a tool. We print "In God We Trust" on our money, but what "god" are we trusting when we live lives characterized by materialistic consumption? To start your day, do you reach for your Bible or do you reach for the Wall Street Journal? Do you spend more time worried about your stock portfolio or how best you can be of service to the Kingdom of God? Or how about this: is your faith characterized by what "blessings" you hope you gain from the Father more than how you can be a blessing to others?

The Heart's Allegiance

The basic philosophy of humanism, as it is defined today, is that people are gods unto themselves. However, human nature is also a slave to the evolutionary philosophy of "survival of the fittest." And how do we effectively define who is the fittest? By the amount of earthly treasure that we horde to ourselves. Even our modern concepts of philanthropy and benevolence in society are defined by the amount of "disposable wealth" we have that we can "graciously" bestow upon others - most often out of our excess. We celebrate large donors who contribute multiple figures of monies towards worthy causes, but rarely give credence to the "widow's mite" offerings that carry more spiritual value as a result of the relative sacrifice that is made. We exalt those who give much, while pushing those who give everything to give more. We entice larger donations with promises of greater benefits to be earned from the larger "sacrifices" given.

The Heart's Deception

Now please hear me clearly, wealth in and of itself is not a sin. Rather it is the obsessive drive to horde money for oneself out of fear and anxiety and a desire for self-preservation that corrupts the heart. The apostle Paul puts it this way:

If anyone advocates a different doctrine and does not agree with sound words, those of our Lord Jesus Christ, and with the doctrine conforming to godliness, he is conceited and understands nothing; but he has a morbid interest in controversial questions and disputes about words, out of which arise envy, strife, abusive language, evil suspicions, and constant friction between men of depraved mind and deprived of the truth, who suppose that godliness is a means of gain. But godliness actually is a means of great gain when accompanied by contentment. For we have brought nothing into the world, so we cannot take anything out of it either. If we have food and covering, with these we shall be content. But those who want to get rich fall into temptation and a snare and many foolish and harmful desires which plunge men into ruin and destruction. For the love of money is a root of all sorts of evil, and some by longing for it have wandered away from the faith and pierced themselves with many griefs. (1 Timothy 6:3-10)

This passage speaks to a few different things as it pertains to wealth. First, it addresses the idea that there are some within the body of Christ who treat godliness as a means of personal gain. They seek to argue the letter of the law yet do not honor the spirit of the law. The totality of the Hebrew law is summed up in two commandments: love God and love other people. However, when we look to God's word as a means to our own personal ends, we tend to distort and corrupt the heart of Scripture. In so doing, we give rise to heresies that detract from the truth of the Kingdom and put ourselves on the throne rather than humbly acknowledging who really is the only one worthy of the Throne of grace. The primary message of the Bible is not about us, but rather it is about God revealing Himself to us, desperately crying out for us to come to Him.

Secondly, the so-called heretical "prosperity gospel" is nothing new. In fact, it was prevalent enough in Paul's day that he specifically called attention to it in his letter to Timothy. He warns that there are teachers who will teach that godliness is a means of personal gain. But he also reminds Timothy that while godliness does bring great gain to the individual on a spiritual level, it must be accompanied by contentment with what God has entrusted us to steward. A lack of contentment is a sign of anxiety and misplaced priorities that put the self before the good of God's kingdom.

Finally, he describes how those who are rich fall into temptation that "plunge men into ruin and destruction." But it's not the fact that they are rich that is the problem. It is when they allow the size of their bank accounts to supersede the size of their vision for the kingdom of God. It's when they allow their love of money to become an idol rather than a tool to be used to further the interest of God's kingdom that the temptation comes and destroys them.

A Heart of Stewardship

One of the most abused scriptures I've seen in recent years is Luke 6:38 that is often taken out of context and quoted as a encouragement to give in expectation of return on Kingdom investment.

"…give, and it will be given to you. Good measure, pressed down, shaken together, running over, will be put into your lap. For with the measure you use it will be measured back to you." – Luke 6:38

This passage is not talking about material blessing or the giving of offerings. In fact, it is very specifically in the context of judgement, condemnation, mercy, and grace towards those who would abuse our own kindness towards them. The passage even ends with the familiar warning against judging without a full clarity of vision by engaging in self-examination ("remove the log from your own eye") before judging another ("remove the speck from your brother's eye"). Be careful not to take a passage of Scripture out of its proper context to support a point of argument that the passage was not intended for.

I happen to have friends and colleagues who I would consider to be wealthy people. But it's not the size of the bank accounts that make them wealthy in my eyes, but rather it is the size of their heart. If your view of your personal wealth is a means of drawing attention to yourself, then your vision extends no further than yourself. However if your view of your personal wealth is as means of being a steward of God's resources for the advancement of His purposes, it makes a world of difference in your vision of life.

Reflection Questions

- What does your daily routine reveal about who or what is mastering your heart?

  ____

  ____

  ____

- Are you using your resources for God's kingdom, or are they using you?

  ____

  ____

  ____

Application Points

- **Start each day with God's Word** - let Scripture shape your heart before the world shapes your desires.
- **Evaluate your giving** - is it out of surplus or sacrificial love? Consider how the widow's offering (Mark 12:41–44) reflects Kingdom values.
- **Reject prosperity thinking** - embrace contentment and generosity as true signs of spiritual maturity (Philippians 4:11–13).

Prayer Prompt

Lord, I confess the ways I have trusted in wealth more than in You. Help me to be a faithful steward of all You've given me—not seeking personal gain, but Kingdom fruit. Teach me to find joy in contentment and to use what I have to bless others in Your name. Amen.

The Security of the Kingdom

"For this reason I say to you, do not be worried about your life, as to what you will eat or what you will drink; nor for your body, as to what you will put on. …For the Gentiles eagerly seek all these things; for your heavenly Father knows that you need all these things. But seek first His kingdom and His righteousness, and all these things will be added to you. So do not worry about tomorrow; for tomorrow will care for itself. Each day has enough trouble of its own." Matthew 6:25-34

As Jesus explains to the crowd gathered on the mountainside that you cannot serve both God and wealth, He immediately and naturally transitions into addressing anxiety and worry, especially in the context of material provision. Most of the crowd were likely poor peasants, languishing beneath the boot of the powerful Roman state. Yet some among them were comparatively wealthy, often as a reward for cooperating with their Roman oppressors. In both cases, whether in poverty or wealth, provision was entangled with fear and anxiety beneath the heel of the Empire. And Jesus' message was meant for both groups.

The Weight of Anxiety

For the poor, His message was clear, but not easy to live out. They were forced to wonder each day where their next meal would come from. Many lived in fear that soldiers might break down their doors to confiscate what little food or possessions they had. Speaking out against Rome meant treason, imprisonment, or loss of property. Thus, the poor lived under a constant shadow of resentment, fear, and anxiety—always uncertain about the next day's provision.

For the wealthy, His message was harder to see and even harder to embrace. Many had secured their comfort through small compromises with Rome. Tax collectors, for example, were viewed as traitors, often enriching themselves at the expense of their neighbors. Driven by fear of losing their status and security, their hearts became tethered to the wealth of the empire rather than the love of God.

True Security in Christ

Where you place your faith will always shape your sense of security. If your trust rests in government, every election cycle will feel like a threat to your stability. If it rests in wealth, your peace will rise and fall with the markets. If it rests in your career, job insecurity will drive you into restlessness or workaholism. If it rests in your family, the inevitable brokenness of human relationships will bring disappointment. If it rests in beauty or status, the passing of time will tempt you to chase artificial solutions that never satisfy.

But none of these things are bad in themselves. Family, vocation, community, and even beauty are good gifts from God. The danger comes when we look to them for what only Christ can provide—our ultimate security, peace, and hope. However, if you place your faith in the immovable Rock of Christ—the firm foundation, the chief cornerstone—then you can know true peace. Jesus never promised a life free from need or difficulty, but He did promise His abiding presence. As He told His disciples before ascending into heaven:

"All authority in heaven and on earth has been given to me. Go therefore and make disciples of all nations, baptizing them in the name of the Father and of the Son and of the Holy Spirit, teaching them to observe all that I have commanded you. And behold, I am with you always, to the end of the age." (Matthew 28:18–20)

The call is simple but profound: Seek first the Kingdom of God and His righteousness. This means a heart of repentance, a mind renewed by His Word, and a life oriented toward His will. It means trusting Him not only for daily bread, but also for eternal security. And it means living on mission—making disciples, knowing that His presence goes with us always. In this way, we find rest, peace, and joy in Him, from now until eternity.

Reflection Questions

- What good gifts in my life am I tempted to rely on for ultimate security instead of trusting in Christ?

  ____

  ____

  ____

- How does remembering Christ's continual presence reshape the way I respond to fear and anxiety?

  ____

  ____

  ____

Application Points

- Thank God for family, work, and daily provision, but remember they are meant to point you back to Him as the true Giver.
- When anxiety rises, practice entrusting those concerns to God in prayer, resting in His care.
- Prioritize spiritual practices—prayer, Scripture, service, and discipleship—that root your heart in God's eternal promises. Schedule time for each of these disciplines as divine appointments.

Prayer Prompt

Father, thank You for the many good gifts You have given me—my family, my work, my daily provision. Help me to cherish them without depending on them for my ultimate security. Teach me to rest in Jesus Christ, my cornerstone, who promises never to leave me. May my heart seek first Your Kingdom and trust fully in Your presence. Amen.

The Judgement of the Kingdom

"Do not judge so that you will not be judged. For in the way you judge, you will be judged; and by your standard of measure, it will be measured to you. Why do you look at the speck that is in your brother's eye, but do not notice the log that is in your own eye? Or how can you say to your brother, 'Let me take the speck out of your eye,' and behold, the log is in your own eye? You hypocrite, first take the log out of your own eye, and then you will see clearly to take the speck out of your brother's eye. Do not give what is holy to dogs, and do not throw your pearls before swine, or they will trample them under their feet, and turn and tear you to pieces." (Matthew 7:1-6)

There is a fine line between judgement and accountability, and it is predicated by a carefully cultivated relationship and personal responsibility. More often than not, when we seek to correct the behavior of another, we can be met with resistance. However, this resistance is mostly due to one thing: you have not cultivated the relationship necessary to develop a safe environment for accountability. In which case, attempts at holding another accountable will be seen as an attitude of judgement. This is why is vitally important that we have a sense of discernment about ourselves and the relationship we have with others before we seek to be an agent of correction and discipline.

Judgement or Accountability

All too often, anyone who feels judged will quote the first verse and leave out the remainder of the verse in an effort to avoid the feelings of correction. The remainder of this passage does not say that we should not hold each other accountable for our sins. However, it does explain that we should exercise self-awareness and discernment before we seek to correct our brothers and sisters. Ensure that your own heart is in the right and that your relationship with that person is in a place that is going to be receptive to the corrective accountability first. If you act of self-righteous indignation, then you will very likely not witness the repentance that is intended. Otherwise, hypocrisy is creeping at the door of your own heart.

On the other hand, we are indeed called to hold one another accountable within the Kingdom for our behavior. James put it this way: "My brothers, if any among you strays from the truth and one turns him back, let him know that he who turns a sinner from the error of his way will save his soul from death and will cover a multitude of sins." (James 5:19) Notice here that James is leveraging the relationship of brotherhood in the course of accountability.

Rooted in Relationship

There are numerous times throughout Scripture that Jesus speaks to holding one another accountable within the Kingdom. But in every case, he encourages self-discernment and leveraging the interpersonal relationship you have with the other. If you do not have a relationship with someone that you are seeking to discipline, how can you expect them to heed your warnings? You wouldn't go about disciplining an unruly child you didn't know or have a relationship with, would you? Of course not! You'd seek out the parent of that child and describe the situation and allow them to exercise the responsibility of discipline because they have the relationship with the child that is more likely to produce repentance.

In the same way, Jesus admonishes us not to pass judgement upon those who are outside of the Kingdom when He says "Do not give what is holy to dogs, and do not throw your pearls before swine, or they will trample them under their feet, and turn and tear you to pieces." In this passage, "dogs" and "swine" are referring to wild packs of animals - wild dogs and wild boars that would roam the countryside seeking to devour everything in their path - scavengers. At first glance, and when taken out of context, it seems like Jesus is being rude here, but you have to consider His audience.

Kingdom Accountability - World Witness

Wild dogs are known to be destructive and untamable, often traveling nocturnally in packs together wreaking havoc on weaker animals and consuming the trash and leftovers of the stronger predators. In fact, during the COVID-19 lockdowns, it was reported that jackals were starting to take over parks in Tel Aviv, Israel at night due to the absence of humans. These packs of wild dogs are not only dangerous to human populations, but are highly territorial and aggressive with one another in their fight for survival. Wild pigs were considered ritually unclean in Jewish society, but also would travel in packs or hordes. In both cases, if you approach these packs alone and try to scare them off or get them to stop their destruction, the entire pack is likely to turn on you, ignore your commands, and attack you instead. Is it any surprise that the same thing happens when we followers of Christ try to correct or discipline those who live outside of the Kingdom?

As Paul once wrote, "For the word of the cross is foolishness to those who are perishing, but to us who are being saved it is the power of God." (1 Corinthians 1:18-25) The commandments of God were written for His people. The Scriptures give us a guide to live by and a standard to hold one another to. However, non-believers who live outside of the Kingdom are not likely to bow to the dictates of Scripture. They live by a different standard - typically the standard of their own humanism that elevates their own self-interest above the interests of God's Kingdom.

Nations do not impose their domestic laws on citizens of other countries when those individuals remain outside their jurisdiction. Each country has authority only within its own borders. However, when a foreign national enters the United States, that person is subject to U.S. law while within its territory. In the same way, when an American travels abroad, he or she must live under the laws of the host nation. If a conflict arises between the laws of two nations, the law of the jurisdiction where the person is physically present generally takes precedence. This principle of jurisdiction underscores the reality that laws only apply where a governing authority has been established.

And the same is true of the Kingdom of God. Just as a nation's laws only apply within its jurisdiction, so the commands of God apply in their fullness to those who live under His reign—those who have entered His Kingdom by faith in Christ. This does not mean we should ignore or withdraw from the world around us. On the contrary, we are called to bear witness to Christ and invite others into His Kingdom. But we must remember that lasting transformation begins not with enforcing Kingdom standards on those who do not yet know the King, but by proclaiming the gospel that changes hearts. Once hearts are transformed by grace, behavior follows. And this heart change is most often nurtured through relationships of trust, where the seed of God's truth can be planted and, in time, bear the fruit of repentance.

Reflection Questions

- When have I been tempted to correct someone without first cultivating a loving relationship?

 ____

 ____

 ____

- How can I reflect Christ's heart so that my correction is received as love rather than judgment?

____

____

____

Application Points

- Before addressing another's sin, prayerfully consider your own motives and spiritual state (Matt 7:3–5).
- Invest in genuine care for others so that correction flows from love, not authority alone.
- Remember that non-believers need Christ's transforming grace more than moral correction – lead with the gospel, not condemnation.

Prayer Prompts

Lord, give me discernment to know when and how to hold others accountable. Guard my heart from hypocrisy or self-righteousness. Help me to build relationships of love and trust so that truth can be spoken with grace. Teach me to reflect Your Kingdom heart in such a way that others are drawn to repentance and to You. Amen.

The Gifts of the Kingdom

"Ask, and it will be given to you; seek, and you will find; knock, and it will be opened to you. For everyone who asks receives, and he who seeks finds, and to him who knocks it will be opened. Or what man is there among you who, when his son asks for a loaf, will give him a stone? Or if he asks for a fish, he will not give him a snake, will he? If you then, being evil, know how to give good gifts to your children, how much more will your Father who is in heaven give what is good to those who ask Him!" (Matthew 7:7-11)

One of the very basic principles of Biblical study is to apply textual context when examining a given passage. Perhaps one of the most blatant examples of a passage of Scripture that is studied out of context and then twisted to fit a humanistic, self-centered agenda is Matthew 7:7-11. Taken in isolation and viewed on the surface without digging into the full context of the passage, it seems to reduce the Almighty and holy God of Creation to a sort of celestial "Santa Claus". Nothing could be farther from the truth.

Kingdom Context

We must remember that in the Sermon on the Mount, Jesus has been describing what it is like to live in the Kingdom of God, to be a citizen of God's domain, and a member of His family, with Him at the head of the family. Repeatedly Jesus has implored His audience to seek God's Kingdom and the will of the Father and has warned against seeking after our own selfish desires and lust that corrupt us. This sets the stage and the mentality in the mind of the audience to give appropriate context for the petitions we bring to the throne of grace.

When we are focused on Kingdom priorities and the fulfillment of God's will in our individual lives, this ultimately transforms our way of thinking as our desires are replaced by His desires. Our hearts become broken for the things that break the heart of God. Our hearts are filled with joy at that which brings joy to the heart of the Father. And it informs our petitions before the throne of grace.

The Father Who Gives Good Gifts

If a child were to go to his father and ask for a poisonous snake as a pet, would a loving and generous father give that child such a gift when requested? Of course not, don't be ridiculous. Just as a father would give a gift to the child that is good for them, they would withhold "gifts" from the child that would prevent them from living their best life, knowing that the request was not in their best interest.

We do not get to define what is "good" for us. That is the prerogative of the Father. He is the one who knows what our future holds. He is the only one who sees beyond what our limited vision is capable of seeing. When we are focused on Kingdom priorities, it changes our petitions to reflect God's desires for His children. The more intimately we know the heart of the Father, the more confidently we can approach the throne of grace knowing our Godly petitions will be granted in the interest of His Kingdom.

It takes boldness and even audacity to approach a king with a personal request. Typically, from a standpoint of human interests in government, the only thing a citizen could rightfully ask the king for is mercy. In some cases, entering into the presence of a king without invitation or announcement would be grounds for execution.

Approach the Throne With Confidence

Such was the plight of Queen Esther as she entered the presence of the King, knowing that to do so could mean certain death (Esther 4:16). However, as Esther had already cultivated a relationship with the king as his queen, and she had found favor in his eyes, Esther was allowed to issue an invitation to fellowship, which he graciously accepted. It was at this dinner that Esther exposed a plot to exterminate the Jewish race. Her genuine relationship with the King gave her the boldness and confidence to approach Him with her request. In so doing, the Jews were saved from certain destruction - preserving God's plan for His people.

As children of the King, we are effectively Princes and Princesses of Creation. Our relationship with the Father gives us the boldness and conviction by which we can approach His throne with our petitions. By virtue of our relationship with the Father we can enter His presence without fear, knowing that He will hear our prayer and grant our desires insomuch that they align with His Kingdom purposes.

Reflection Questions

- How have I sometimes approached God as if He were meant to fulfill my will rather than shape me to His?

  ____

  ____

  ____

- In what ways does knowing God as a loving Father give me confidence to bring Him my needs?

  ____

  ____

  ____

Application Points

- Spend time in Scripture and prayer so that your petitions reflect God's Kingdom priorities, not just personal wants.

- Remember that God withholds what will harm us and gives what will grow us in Christlikeness.
- Approach God boldly, not in fear, because through Christ you are His child and heir (Rom 8:15–17).

Prayer Prompt

Father, thank You that You are not a distant ruler or a celestial gift-dispenser, but a loving Father who knows what is best for me. Align my desires with Your Kingdom. Teach me to trust Your wisdom when You say yes, when You say no, and when You say wait. Give me confidence to approach You boldly, knowing I am Your child through Christ. Amen.

The Rule of the Kingdom

"In everything, therefore, treat people the same way you want them to treat you, for this is the Law and the Prophets." Matthew 7:12

Jesus and the Law itself have boldly explained that the greatest commandment is to "Love the Lord your God with all heart and all your soul and with all your mind." (Matthew 22:37) However, Jesus elevated the second greatest commandment to be a natural outgrowth of the first "Love your neighbor as yourself." (Matthew 22:39) In effect, He was making this declaration: "Your love for God is demonstrated by your love for His greatest creation - people."

Accountability and the Golden Rule

Love, as defined by Matthew 22, is the Greek word agapao. Love is not a noun in that passage, but it is a verb. A word of action that demonstrates a deeper inner condition. The word agapáō (ἀγαπάω) in the imperfect tense implies incompletion, or more appropriately a continuous act without end. The word in this tense is used 144 times in the New Testament over 110 verses. It is perhaps the most important word in all of Scripture because it defines the heart of God towards His creation and provides us with a lens through which to observe His actions towards us. He treats us with love, because He desires for us to love Him. He disciplines us in order to draw us back to Him. He seeks to withhold from us that which would make us distant from Him. And He loves us enough to give us a choice to love Him, yet not without making the consequences of such abandonment clear. This demonstration of His great love for us is His example of how we are to treat one another.

We speak the truth in love to one another, not to be a herald of judgement, but to be a beacon of grace, guidance, restoration, and love. We ought to expect the same from others around us. Yet all too often, we either speak judgement against one another, which is the antithesis of God's desire for us. Judgement is born out of hatred, but accountability is born out of love. Judgement destroys hope; accountability provides restoration. And it's very easy to blur the lines between the two - as both the one delivering discipline and the one receiving it. In both cases, it is because our vision is obscured by our own inner condition. That is why Jesus warns earlier to examine your own heart before seeking to provide discipline and extend accountability.

We speak of the Golden Rule more often in defensive terms, but the tone and tense of the commandment is active and on the offense, rather than defense. Most of the time when we hear anyone bring up the Golden Rule, it is to defend their own condition and plea for grace and mercy, or rather more appropriately ignorance. However, the Golden Rule is stated in such a way as to be proactive, rather than reactive. It's imperative as opposed to submissive. The Rule doesn't say "Do not treat others the same way you do not want them to treat you." That's passive and barely even reactive.

The Moral Lawgiver

So how ought we to treat one another in love? What does that look like? We serve one another. We sacrifice for one another. We respect one another in spite of our differences. We recognize one another as one of God's children, created in His image for His purposes. To treat one another as we want to be treated is to recognize our God-ordained design as His image bearers. Sometimes that means discipline, but more importantly that means grace.

When we abuse one another, are we treating each other the way that we want to be treated? How ridiculous a proposition! But every day we see it over and over again. Domestic violence continues to invade our homes. Human trafficking continues to rise in every corner of the globe. We treat one another as objects for our own gain, rather than as God's children designed to be loved.

When we reduce humanity to nothing more than a batch of cells put together by mere random chance with no clear purpose, it is inevitable that we see not only ourselves as a god unto ourselves, but others as objects to be used to further our own agendas and animalistic desires. Evolution does not solve for the moral imperative to love. In fact, anyone who tells you that morality is ingrained in each of us without the need of God or creation, is borrowing capital from God Himself. Moral law directly implies that there is a law giver that defines that law. In order for a moral law to be universally applied, it must come from a law giver that stands outside of that universe. Whether we choose to accept that God is our moral law-giver or not, does not negate our responsibility to His law. Ignorance of the law is no excuse for breaking the law in American society. The same basic principle applies in the spiritual realm as well.

The Virtue of Humility

The greatest virtue that extends from love is humility. Humility recognizes our place before the throne of grace, whereas pride seeks to elevate our place to sit upon the throne that is not ours. James, the younger brother of Jesus, states "Do you think that the Scripture speaks to no purpose: 'He jealously desires the Spirit which He has made to dwell in us'? But He gives a greater grace. Therefore it says 'God is opposed to the proud, but gives grace to the humble.' Submit therefore to God. Resist the devil and he will flee from you." (James 4:5-7)

Humbly stand your ground in love for one another. Resist the temptation to stand in pride against one another. Submit your desires to God's heart and let His Spirit transform you. When we learn what it means to humbly submit to Him in trust and love, then, and only then, will we ever truly understand how to love one another.

Reflection Questions

- How does my love for others reveal the depth of my love for God?

  ____

  ____

  ____

- Where might I be tempted to judge instead of lovingly holding others accountable?

  ____

  ____

  ____

Application Points

- Seek ways to serve and sacrifice for others daily as an overflow of your love for God.
- Correct others only from a place of humility and grace, with restoration as the goal.
- Daily submit your desires to God, asking His Spirit to shape your heart so you can love as He loves.

Prayer Prompt

Lord, teach me to love You with all my heart, soul, and mind, and to love my neighbor as myself. Help me to resist pride and judgment, and instead extend grace and accountability in love. Shape my heart with humility so that my life reflects Your Kingdom love. Amen.

The Gate of the Kingdom

"Enter through the narrow gate; for the gate is wide and the way is broad that leads to destruction, and there are many who enter through it. For the gate is small and the way is narrow that leads to life, and there are few who find it." Matthew 7:13-14

One of the most beautiful places in the world is Tuscany, Italy. There is one town that is particularly interesting - Monteriggioni. It is a very small town situated on a hilltop about 20 km northwest of Siena and an hour south of Florence, the home of one of Italy's greatest poets, Dante Alighieri. Monteriggioni is known for its medieval fortress design with a wall that encloses the town and its high watchtowers. There is a singular road that encircles the town, and only a single road through a single gate that allows entrance. The commune and its majestic watchtowers were the inspiration of the circle of giants that protected the entrance to Hell in Dante's classic work "Inferno", part of his Divine Comedy trilogy.

The Gate to Monteriggioni

Monteriggioni is not a town that many people immediately think of when they consider their travels to Italy. The flashier fashion mecca of Milan, the historical center of the Roman Empire in Rome, the Grand Canal of Venice, and Renaissance muses of Florence all draw far more attention to the holiday traveler. Even Siena and Pisa draw more attention in the Tuscan region than this quiet little out of the way hilltop paradise that sits less than a mile from the main road. But those who visit often stand in awe of the majestic beauty of its ancient walls and view of the quiet, serene Tuscan valley.

The entrance gate to Monteriggioni, also known as the Porta Franca, is quite narrow to enter. In fact, it is so narrow, that a motorized vehicle can barely fit through the entrance, so most automobiles are forbidden entrance and must park outside of the fortressed community. The only vehicles allowed inside of the town are official vehicles for emergency services. In medieval times, entrance to the town was only allowed with the permission of the city magistrate/authority. What an interesting illustration of what it means to enter the gates of the Kingdom through "the narrow gate."

I've once heard it said that the fact that there is a "highway to Hell" and a "stairway to Heaven" says a lot about the population at the destination. What makes entrance into the Kingdom of God so difficult is not so much the path, but rather the choice and the requirements for entrance. You can see a narrow gate from a distance and recognize whether or not you can fit through it, and many once faced with this decision choose instead an easier, more comfortable doorway - a doorway that appeals to pride and self-sufficiency. The path to such a doorway is wide and smooth without a steep climb that requires effort.

But the path to the entrance to the Kingdom is narrow. It's difficult and prone to stumbling. It's a climb up a hill, on top of which stands a cross. The cross of the hill of Golgotha. The crucifixion cross of Christ, upon which is nailed the sins of the world. It is by that cross that God fulfills the promise to "destroy the wisdom of the wise and the cleverness of the clever." (1 Corinthians 1:19)

One illustration for the cross that one can use as an evangelistic tool is this: *it is the intersection of God's judgement, from the heights of His holiness to the depths of our lowliness, with the crossbeam of His love on the one hand and mercy on the other, as His arms are forever stretched out waiting to embrace you.* This picture of grace is not an easy one to accept because our human nature and humanistic philosophies require human effort, but with limited sacrifice. Humanism appeals to human pride by elevating mankind to the point of godhood.

One striking example of humanistic glory tempered by pride is Lorenzo de' Medici, known as *Il Magnifico*. He was a great patron of the arts—supporting scholars, painters, poets, and sculptors—including Botticelli, Leonardo da Vinci, and Michelangelo. Yet, as much as his achievements drew admiration, they also masked something deeper. As Hannah S. Bowers observes, "Lorenzo used his charm and perceptive leadership to pursue his own desires. In the end, he was viewed by contemporaries as Plato's 'perfect man'."* (Bowers, 2012) It was this very mixture of talent, influence, and unchecked ambition that sowed seeds of corruption—within human hearts, in the political sphere, and even within the Church itself. Even Savonarola, who railed against corruption, fell to pride and power. Yet their failures stirred the conscience of Martin Luther, who rediscovered the narrow way of grace by faith – not indulgences or human achievement.

But the gate to the Kingdom is a simple, unassuming gate. It simply beckons you to enter, but it requires laying aside your pride and submitting to the authority of God. It requires taking a step of faith to climb the hill of Calvary and bowing at the foot of the cross. It requires leaving behind the easy path of the highway and taking the path that is difficult, the path of obedience. The path of faith. And it is not an unreasonable or blind faith.

Paul encourages us to "Not be conformed to the ways of this world, but be transformed by the renewing of your mind, so that you may prove what the will of God is, that which is good and acceptable and perfect." (Romans 12:2) Our discipline starts with our mind, transforming the way that we think of this world. Recognizing that our way has lead to our own destruction for too long and that it is time that we try a new way. A more difficult way, but a more rewarding way. An impossible path on our own, but a path that He will walk with us because in the end, He is the gate. He is the door. He Himself is the entrance to the Kingdom. He beckons you to lay aside your pride and your self-sufficiency and rest in Him. Today and forevermore.

* Hannah S. Bowers, *"Lorenzo de Medici: A True Renaissance Man,"* *CoffeeshopThinking*, March 30, 2012, https://coffeeshopthinking.wordpress.com/2012/03/30/lorenzo-de-medici-a-true-renaissance-man/

Reflection Questions

- What "wide gates" of pride, comfort, or self-reliance tempt me away from following Christ through the narrow gate?

  ____

  ____

  ____

- How does remembering Jesus Himself as the true Gate strengthen my trust and obedience?

  ____

  ____

  ____

Application Points

- Lay down pride: Confess areas where you have trusted in your own strength or status instead of Christ.
- Make daily choices of obedience, even when they are costly or uncomfortable.
- Let the love and mercy of Christ at Calvary reshape your values and desires.

Prayer Prompt

Lord Jesus, You are the narrow gate and the only way into the Father's Kingdom. I confess the times I have chosen the easier, wider path of pride and comfort. Teach me to walk the harder way of humility, obedience, and faith. Renew my mind, strengthen my heart, and lead me daily to the cross where Your mercy and love meet me. Amen.

The Fruit of the Kingdom

"Beware of the false prophets, who come to you in sheep's clothing, but inwardly are ravenous wolves. You will know them by their fruits. Grapes are not gathered from thorn bushes nor figs from thistles, are they? So every good tree bears good fruit, but the bad tree bears bad fruit. A good tree cannot produce bad fruit, nor can a bad tree produce good fruit. Every tree that does not bear good fruit is cut down and thrown into the fire. So then, you will know them by their fruits." - Matthew 7:15-20

We've all heard the phrase "A wolf in sheep's clothing." If you've ever wondered the origin of that phrase, then here you have it. Contextually speaking, Jesus is referring to false prophets and teachers. These individuals who prey on the ignorant with what sounds like wisdom, but is in fact intentional deceit designed to satisfy their own appetites and lust for power. If you ever hear a preacher or teacher or anyone claiming to be a prophet or apostle, but their teaching is focused more on themselves, on individuals, and anything other than the Kingdom of God, then you can rest assured they are sowing bad seed that produces poisonous fruit. It will make you sick of yourself, distract you from His mission, and ultimately kill your joy.

Recognizing Wolves Among the Flock

When members of the Secret Service are taught how to recognize counterfeit money, they are not shown fake bills. They are made to study the real bills so that they can more readily recognize anything that doesn't measure up to the standard of truth. In data science, there is a principle that we adhere to in order to ascertain if the data that we are analyzing is accurate - the principle of the source of truth. Anything that violates or doesn't measure up to the source of truth is considered invalid analysis and thus requires re-examination. The same applies when recognizing false teaching.

The True Measure of Truth

What is the fruit of a true prophet/teacher that is humbly tuned to the word of God? There are certain hallmarks of Biblical teaching and Biblical interpretation that will ring true every time. There are in fact several factors that we must consider in terms of how to identify a false teacher, but I will sum them up by identifying what identifies the teaching of the true gospel.

First, and foremost, the true gospel acknowledges the Jesus is the ONLY way to the Father. He is THE way, THE truth, and THE life, and no one comes to the Father except through Him. (John 14:6) Anyone who adds themselves or another teacher to this truth is a liar and the truth is not in them. Any religious creed or principle that states you must follow a specific prophet or teacher or leader in addition to Jesus in order to be in the Kingdom is false and I urge you to run the opposite direction.

Secondly, any teaching that is contrary to God's established canon of Scripture is not to be trusted. The canon of Scripture was closed no later than 100 AD, and there are more than 7000 original manuscripts – including Greek manuscripts, partial fragments, and later copies – that can attest to the authenticity of this claim. The Old Testament canon was widely accepted and established well before the 1st century AD. This is testified to by the Jewish historian Flavius Josephus (William Whiston, trans., Flavius Josephus against Apion, Vol. 1, in Josephus, Complete Works, Grand Rapids, Kregel, 1960, p. 8). The New Testament canon was well established and first testified to by the Muratorian Fragment dated to 170 AD, but this list of apostolic writings was considered closed by the Synod of Hippo in 393 AD, as well as the Council of Carthage in 397 AD.

Books that were originally considered canon but found to be written too late to be authoritative or were theologically out of line with apostolic teaching were discarded.

As Paul wrote to Timothy, "All Scripture is inspired by God and profitable for teaching, for reproof, for correction, for training in righteousness; so that the man of God may be adequate, equipped for every good work." (2 Timothy 3:16-17) While Paul was primarily referring to the Old Testament canon of his day, the apostle Peter considered Paul's epistles and other apostolic writings to be equal to the Old Testament canon:

"Therefore, beloved, since you look for these things, be diligent to be found by Him in peace, spotless and blameless, and regard the patience of our Lord as salvation; just as also our beloved brother Paul, according to the wisdom given him, wrote to you, as also in all his letters, speaking in them of these things, in which are some things hard to understand, which the untaught and unstable distort, as they do also the rest of the Scriptures, to their own destruction. You therefore, beloved, knowing this beforehand, be on your guard so that you are not carried away by the error of unprincipled men and fall from your own steadfastness, but grow in the grace and knowledge of our Lord and Savior Jesus Christ. To Him be the glory, both now and to the day of eternity. Amen." *(2 Peter 3:14-18)*

Fruit of the Spirit / Deeds of the Flesh

Finally, the teachings of the Kingdom produce Godly fruit that is easily recognizable in the heart of the believer. "But the fruit of the Spirit is love, joy, peace, patience, kindness, goodness, faithfulness, gentleness, self-control; against such things there is no law." (Galatians 5:22-23) Any teaching that produces fruit contrary to this is false.

In fact, just prior to this list of the Fruit of the Spirit, Paul describes those characteristics that stand out as the fruit of counterfeit teaching and a counterfeit life: "Now the deeds of the flesh are evident, which are: immorality, impurity, sensuality, idolatry, sorcery, enmities, strife, jealousy, outbursts of anger, disputes, dissensions, factions, envying, drunkenness, carousing, and things like these, of which I forewarn you, just as I have forewarned you, that ***those who practice such things will not inherit the kingdom of God***." (Galatians 5:19-21) If any teaching from the pulpit or from a Bible Study class or from any form of mentorship or "disciplining" produces this kind of fruit in your own heart or the heart of others, then it is incumbent upon us as believers to admonish and correct such teaching in the interest of the truth for the sake of the Kingdom.

The danger therein lies when we mix the fruit of the unrighteousness with the fruit of the Spirit and produce a sort of "wolf in sheep's clothing" theology that creates confusion and deception. For example, when we treat the name of Jesus like it is some sort of magical incantation by misinterpreting the scriptures that say "whatever you ask in my name, I will do it" (John 14:13-14), we are mixing sorcery into our prayers when Jesus' words there was intended to beckon submission to the will of the Father, not bend the Father to our will. Another example would be the practice of venerating religious relics or props as having some sort of mystical power to heal or grant wishes. This is nothing more than a form of idolatry masquerading as devotion.

Personally, I invite challenges to anything that I teach. If I am wrong, then please, I humbly accept such correction. But be forewarned, that if you do choose to challenge what I do teach, come prepared with a Biblical substantiation for your point of view. This is the standard by which I seek to measure anything that I teach and it is the standard that I will hold you to if you choose to bring correction.

Hold fast to the principles of truth. Know the fruit of the teaching that you adhere to. Measure everything against the totality of Scripture within the established context of Scripture itself. Be on the alert of the wolf that prowls within the flock, seeking to divide and conquer. Examine yourself to ensure that you are not that wolf yourself.

Reflection Questions

- In what ways can believers guard their hearts and churches from being influenced by false teachers who "appear" godly but bear bad fruit?

  ____

  ____

  ____

- What "fruit" do you see being produced in your own life and community—does it reflect the Spirit's work or the world's influence?

  ____

  ____

  ____

Application Points

- **Test Every Teaching by Scripture:** Develop the discipline of examining all teaching through the lens of God's Word, not personality, emotion, or popularity (Acts 17:11).
- **Discern the Fruit:** Look beyond eloquent words or charisma - evaluate whether a teacher's life and message produce Christlike fruit in others.
- **Stay Rooted in Truth:** Study Scripture daily to strengthen your spiritual discernment; spiritual deception thrives where biblical illiteracy grows.

Prayer Prompt

Lord Jesus, Thank You for being the Good Shepherd who protects Your flock. Grant me discernment to recognize truth from error, humility to receive correction, and courage to stand firm in Your Word. Let the fruit of Your Spirit grow in me so that I might reflect Your truth in love. Guard my heart from deceit and use me to build up Your church in grace and truth. Amen.

The Identity of the Kingdom

"Not everyone who says to Me, 'Lord, Lord,' will enter the kingdom of heaven, but he who does the will of My Father who is in heaven will enter. Many will say to Me on that day, 'Lord, Lord, did we not prophesy in Your name, and in Your name cast out demons, and in Your name perform many miracles?' And then I will declare to them, 'I never knew you; DEPART FROM ME, YOU WHO PRACTICE LAWLESSNESS.'" – Matthew 7:21-23

Much has been said and written about our current American political climate and the apparent divisiveness that has characterized our national discourse over the last 20 years. We have seen bitterness and anger manifest itself in unimaginable ways. From racial discord to gender inequities to identity politics, we have been witnessing and continue to witness the undermining of the rule of law in the name of humanism driven by emotion rather than submission to divine truth.

God did not make a mistake when He created you. He created you with a design in mind that suits His purposes for His Kingdom to our good. He designed you with special care and knit you together in the womb to prepare you for what He has in store for you in terms of His goodness and grace. We argue this until Kingdom come but the fact remains that there are only two genders: male and female. And you were genetically designed to be one or the other. No amount of superficial surgical intervention can change the fact that your genetic makeup, the building blocks of who God designed you to be, is immutable. It cannot be changed. You will always have either XX chromosomes as a female or XY chromosomes as a male. Gender is defined biologically, not emotionally.

True Discipleship: More than Words

In the same manner, just because you identify yourself as a Christian does not necessarily mean that you really are. Many people mistake a momentary decision for lasting discipleship—but salvation is proven over time through a life transformed by obedience. And the spiritual "genetic" makeup of who you are is not defined by your emotional responses to the gospel message. The only identity transformation that is part of our human design is your spiritual identity, and it is defined by the absence or the presence of the Spirit of God living within you. And the evidence of the His presence and His transformation of your mind and heart is demonstrated to the extent of your obedience.

In our democracy, some people refuse to acknowledge elected leaders, yet their denial doesn't nullify those leaders' authority. In the same way, denying Jesus' authority doesn't change the fact that He is Lord of all. And you can scream to the Heavens that Jesus is not Lord all you want, but eventually you will bend a knee to him and confess that He is indeed Lord:

"So that at the name of Jesus every knee will bow, of those who are in heaven and on earth and under the earth, and that every tongue will confess that Jesus Christ is Lord, to the glory of God the Father." (Philippians 2:10-11)

Known By Christ

It is an inescapable truth. And you can live your life in this world as you choose, but when that time comes, it won't be what you know or even who you know that saves you. It will come down to Who knows you. And Jesus makes it clear that His knowledge of you is predicated on His Spirit living in you to perform the work of righteousness in this world. Miracles can be counterfeited. We can even speak Biblical truth to our hearts' content. But if we don't live our lives in a way that is characterized by His grace, then it is all in vain.

"This is the message we have heard from Him and announce to you, that God is Light, and in Him there is no darkness at all. If we say that we have fellowship with Him and yet walk in the darkness, we lie and do not practice the truth; but if we walk in the Light as He Himself is in the Light, we have fellowship with one another, and the blood of Jesus His Son cleanses us from all sin. If we say that we have no sin, we are deceiving ourselves and the truth is not in us. If we confess our sins, He is faithful and righteous to forgive us our sins and to cleanse us from all unrighteousness. If we say that we have not sinned, we make Him a liar and His word is not in us." (1 John 1:5-10)

I beg you to examine your heart and mind and always be re-examining yourself. Measure your life against the standard of God's Word. Let His word be the plumb line that determines how straight the path is that you are walking. Your citizenship in Heaven is purchased by His blood, but it is evidenced by your submission to His law. Examine yourself but do so in the light of grace. The same Lord who calls us to obedience also promises forgiveness and renewal to all who confess their sins and trust in Him. Our assurance rests not in our perfection, but in His perfect righteousness.

Reflection Questions

- What does it truly mean for Jesus to "know" you, and how does that relationship reveal itself in daily obedience?

  ____

  ____

  ____

- How can Christians maintain both conviction and compassion when confronting cultural beliefs that contradict God's design?

  ____

  ____

  ____

Application Points

- **Pursue Obedience, Not Just Profession:** Faith in Christ must result in transformation and surrender to His will (John 14:15; 1 John 2:3–6).
- **Anchor Your Identity in God's Design:** Reject cultural confusion by affirming that both your physical and spiritual identity are gifts from a wise and purposeful Creator (Genesis 1:27).
- **Examine Your Heart Regularly:** Continually measure your life against Scripture to ensure your walk aligns with the truth you profess (2 Corinthians 13:5).

Prayer Prompt

Father in Heaven, Thank You for creating me in Your image and calling me into fellowship with Your Son. Search my heart and reveal any false confidence or hidden sin that keeps me from walking in Your truth. Teach me to live in humble obedience, not relying on empty words but on the transforming power of Your Spirit. Let my life be evidence that I truly belong to You. In Jesus' name, Amen.

The Foundation of the Kingdom

"Therefore everyone who hears these words of Mine and acts on them, may be compared to a wise man who built his house on the rock. And the rain fell, and the floods came, and the winds blew and slammed against that house; and yet it did not fall, for it had been founded on the rock. Everyone who hears these words of Mine and does not act on them, will be like a foolish man who built his house on the sand. The rain fell, and the floods came, and the winds blew and slammed against that house; and it fell—and great was its fall."
Matthew 7:24-27

As a child growing up in southeast Louisiana, my family and I would often make a summer trip over to the beach on the Gulf of Mexico at Gulfport, MS. This vacation would typically occur during May, well before the height of hurricane season that would come in July and August. One of the joys of these beach excursions, which is by no means unique, was playing in the sand and building sand forts and castles.

Now I was no expert or artisan when it came to building my little sand castles. And this was long before the days of plastic molds and hyper-realistic displays of sand castle mastery. It was a simple time of fun and frivolity. Due to the nature of molding the sand to fit my own image, I would build my little castles closer to the edge of the water, because the wet sand would hold together better than the dry sand that would slip through my fingers so easily. Of course, by the end of the day, with the inevitable ebb and flow of the tides, the incoming waters would eventually wash away my masterpiece, leaving no trace of my creativity.

At the time, there was a small piece of historical nostalgia that always struck me. There was a little gift shop built out of a tugboat that had been washed up across the coastal road during Hurricane Camille in 1969. It was the result of a 24 foot storm surge that washed in over the entirety of the Mississippi Gulf Coast. The gift shop was later destroyed by Category 4 Hurricane Katrina and developers have since demolished the rusting tugboat in 2008.

Storms Are Inevitable; Foundations Matter

At the time, Hurricane Camille was only the third Category 5 hurricane to ever reach landfall in the continental US. Since then, only 2 other hurricanes have reached landfall as a Category 5 - Andrew in 1992, and Michael in 2018. Camille was also one of the most devastating storms on record resulting in 259 deaths and over $1.42 billion in damages (equivalent to $9.9 billion in 2019).

If there is one thing I learned growing up near the Gulf Coast, it is this: damaging storms are inevitable. They come and they go and they leave death and destruction in their wake. It is with this in mind that I recall that my father every year would pick up a hurricane tracking map from the local Cracker Barrel, which was nothing more than a convenience store at that time, before their rebranding as a Southern staple restaurant. He would meticulously track the storms across the Atlantic and the Caribbean and if the storm would make its way into the Gulf, the real preparations would begin.

Trash cans would be cleaned and filled with fresh water. Fresh batteries would be gathered and our hurricane oil lamp would be brought out to the kitchen table. Non-perishable foods would be stored and radios would be checked for functionality. Flashlights would be located and ensured they were conveniently accessible. With the approaching storm, we always knew to expect at least a couple of days being trapped on our hill due to rising waters at the creek below our home, and no electricity for at least a week. Being prepared for the storm made life a little more bearable without the usual comforts of modern technology that the storm would take away.

The storms of life are also inevitable and they will often leave immense destruction behind them. A job lost. A spouse becomes sick. A child runs away. A friend dies. Suffering is a part of life and a symptom of the corruption of creation wrought by the entrance of sin into the world. However, when we are prepared for the certainty of pain and the reality of suffering in the world, we can rest knowing that our lives can withstand the storm because we have built our lives on the rock of obedience to the Word of God and teachings of Jesus.

If you examine the construction of European castles, you will find a couple of different things. Castles that are built in low-lying areas, or even on beaches, are typically left in ruins. However, fortresses that are built on rocky cliffs, hills, and mountains have stood for centuries, unabated by the forces of nature and the attacks of enemies. In every case, the strength of the engineering of the foundation of these castles that has been credited with their longevity and survival.

This basic function of architecture is still employed in construction today. I have a friend and brother named Matt, who is a home builder. He once described the process of building a new home by starting with the foundation. Not only would his team lay out the concrete base, but they would dig deep into the bedrock of the ground and place pillars beneath the foundation in order to solidify the base and prevent against foundation damage from ground settling once the remainder of the house is built. Otherwise, foundation damage can lead to much bigger problems with the home, resulting in weakened physical integrity that could lead to diminished home value, elevated utility bills, and costly repairs later.

Refuge in Christ's Firm Foundation

The foundation of the Christian life is more than simply a pronouncement of faith in Jesus as the Savior. The true and complete foundation is submission to His Lordship in our lives. "Everyone who hears these words of Mine and acts on them, may be compared to a wise man who built his house on the rock." (Matthew 7:24) The rock of His Lordship is what makes Him our Messiah, the Christ. As the Son of God, He inherits the same authority as the Father. It is here that we can find shelter from the storm and the dangers of this life:

> He who dwells in the shelter of the Most High
> Will abide in the shadow of the Almighty.
> I will say to the Lord, "My refuge and my fortress,
> My God, in whom I trust!"
> For it is He who delivers you from the snare of the trapper
> And from the deadly pestilence.
> He will cover you with His pinions,
> And under His wings you may seek refuge;
> His faithfulness is a shield and bulwark. **(Psalm 91:1-4)**

Reflection Questions

- In what ways does my current response to suffering reveal what my life is truly built upon?

  ____

  ____

  ____

- What specific teachings of Jesus do I hear often but struggle to put into practice?

  ____

  ____

  ____

Application Points

- **Identify one area of life where obedience to Christ has been neglected** (speech, relationships, finances, habits) and take one concrete step toward alignment with His commands this week.

  ____

  ____

  ____

- **Memorize Matthew 7:24-25** as a reminder that obedience is the pathway to stability in the storms of life.

  ____

  ____

  ____

- **Evaluate the foundations of your daily rhythms** (prayer, Scripture reading, church community) and strengthen one of them intentionally.

  ____

  ____

  ____

Prayer Prompt

Father, strengthen my heart to build my life on the words of Your Son. Help me not only to hear Your truth but to obey it with trust and gratitude. When the storms of life rise, keep me anchored in Christ, my Rock and my Refuge. Amen.

The Authority of the Kingdom

"When Jesus had finished these words, the crowds were amazed at His teaching; for He was teaching them as one having authority, and not as their scribes." - Matthew 7:28-29

In 2018, my bride Sara and I celebrated our 20th wedding anniversary with a trip to what has become one of our favorite places in the world - Italy. For this trip, that I secretly arranged for us and presented to her for Christmas 2017, I planned excursions around places and sites that carried personal significance to us both. I have personally always been fascinated with the history of the Roman Empire, as well as the religious significance of the Church in Rome. I've also held a passing interest in the Italian Renaissance of Florence, but nothing compared to Sara's interest due to her passion for art and the masterpieces of Michelangelo Buonorotti.

Standing Amazed Before the Masters

As part of this trip, we got to explore the Flavian Amphitheatre (more commonly known as the Colosseo or Colosseum), the Trevi Fountain, and the Vatican Museums. We stood in awe of the magnificent paintings of Michelangelo in the Sistine Chapel. I finally got to feast my eyes on one of my favorite paintings - Raphael's School of Athens. But nothing in Rome compared to the tear-filled awe that we experienced when we stood before Michelangelo's Pieta. The lifelike marble carving of the Virgin Mary cradling the crucified body of Jesus as only a mother could. The realism captured by Michelangelo as one viewed this sculpture was striking in that you felt as if you could reach out and touch the crucified body of our Lord. The taught muscle and soft skin harkened to the darkest day in the history of the world when mankind killed the Creator in the name of self-centered authoritarianism.

For me, the rest of St. Peter's was dull by comparison, although still fascinating to witness. As our trip continued to Florence, we marveled at the magnificent architecture of San Giovanni's Baptistry and the Santa Maria del Fiore Cathedral, more commonly known as the Duomo. The site of the infamous Pazzi conspiracy that claimed the life of Giuliano de Medici and wounded his brother, Lorenzo "Il Magnifico" de Medici. As we explored the city, I stood in awe at the foot of a memorial to one of my own personal literary heroes, Dante Alighieri, author of The Divine Comedy, outside of the Basilica de Santa Croce. This relatively simply basilica (compared to the Duomo), is the final resting place of such famous names as Galileo Galilei, Enrico Fermi, Rossini, Niccolo Machiavelli, Giorgio Vasari, and Michelangelo Buonorotti. We toured this magnificent basilica during our second trip to Florence in September 2019 and we stood in awe in the presence of these great artists and famed men.

While in Florence, we toured the Accademia, home of Michelangelo's famed sculpture, the David, carved from a neglected piece of marble that was left for scrap for decades. We toured the Ufizzi Museum where we observed Sandro Botticelli's masterful works Primavera and Birth of Venus, and we stood in amazement at the beauty captured by this artist of his muse, Simonetta Vespucci. From the Piazza Michelangelo, we had the opportunity to witness the beautiful, breathtaking landscape view of Florence as it nestled along the flowing River Arno. Imagine with me the awe that we experienced and then multiply that by the factor of standing in the presence of the authority of Almighty God has He taught the truths of the Kingdom from a simple hillside.

Standing Amazed Before The Master

The crowds were amazed at His teaching, not because of eloquent words, but because He taught with authority, unlike the teaching of the scribes. He was more than just a breath of fresh air. Here was a man who was different, who was teaching the Scriptures in way that the foremost experts were incapable of teaching. He was teaching the Scriptures in a way that made God and His Kingdom accessible to them like nothing they have ever heard before.

The word for "amazed" in this verse is a Greek word "ekplesso", which means "to strike out or expel by a blow." It carries with it the connotation of a sudden sense of astonishment as opposed to a sense of fanciful wonder. It's as if the Spirit of God Himself struck the hearts of the hearers in a way to open their eyes and ears to see and hear Himself in a new way. The word is also the same root word for "explosion". In essence, God's word exploded in their hearts anew.

When we truly recognize the authority of God as expressed in His word, the inevitable result is an explosion of realization that Jesus is truly someone different. He's greater than the greatest experts of Biblical exegesis that have ever lived. His wisdom is higher and His grace runs deeper than anything we have ever experienced or ever will apart from a relationship with Him. But we must be willing to open our hearts to the majesty that is His word that is backed by His divine authority.

Just as Michelangelo and Botticelli were considered the foremost masters of sculpture and painting of their day, Jesus is the Master of the Kingdom that we will all one day stand in awe and amazement at the authority that He wields from the Word. There is no painting, sculpture, or architectural wonder of this world that can compare to the majestic wonder of standing in the presence of Jesus as He open our hearts and minds to the truth of His word.

Charles Gabriel is credited with having written over 7000 hymns and songs over the course of his lifetime. One of the most prolific hymnist of his day, Gabriel grew up as a farm boy in Iowa. He learned to play music on a simple reed organ in his home as a child. As a young adult, he began teaching, writing, composing, and editing song collections for some of the leading gospel song publishers of the day.

One day he read a poem by E.O. Excell, that was published in 1905. The words of the poem struck him to his core as Excell portrayed the joy of observing Jesus in the Garden of Gethsemane, sweating drops like blood as he prayed on the night of His betrayal. Within moments, he penned a new hymn:

> Verse 1:
> I stand amazed in the presence
> of Jesus the Nazarene,
> and wonder how he could love me,
> a sinner, condemned unclean.
> Verse 2:
> For me it was in the garden
> he prayed, "Not my will, but thine,"
> He had no tears for his own griefs,
> but sweat-drops of blood for mine.
> Refrain:
> How marvelous! How wonderful!
> and my song shall ever be;
> How marvelous! How wonderful!
> is my Savior's love to me!

Reflection Questions

- When have I last experienced genuine awe at the authority of Jesus and the power of His Word?

  ____

  ____

  ____

- What parts of Christ's teaching do I hear regularly but fail to submit to with a heart of worship and obedience?

____

____

____

Application Points

- **Set aside intentional time this week to read a Gospel passage slowly**, asking the Lord to help you recognize anew the authority and beauty of Jesus.
- **Invite the Spirit to expose areas of resistance** in your heart where Christ's authority is acknowledged intellectually but not embraced practically.
- Memorize Matthew 7:28-29 or the refrain of "I Stand Amazed in the Presence" as a way to reorient your heart toward worship throughout the day.

Prayer Prompt

Lord Jesus, open my eyes to behold the wonder of Your authority and the beauty of Your Word. Strike my heart with fresh amazement at who You are, and teach me to receive Your truth with humility and joy. Make my life a testimony to Your greatness, and let my worship overflow from a heart amazed in Your presence. Amen.

Establishing the Kingdom

So when they had come together, they were asking Him, saying, "Lord, is it at this time You are restoring the kingdom to Israel?" He said to them, "It is not for you to know times or epochs which the Father has fixed by His own authority; but you will receive power when the Holy Spirit has come upon you; and you shall be My witnesses both in Jerusalem, and in all Judea and Samaria, and even to the remotest part of the earth." - Acts 1:6-8

Three years have passed since Jesus delivered the Sermon on the Mount in which He proclaimed everything that the Kingdom of God would be like. While it is widely believed by many scholars that the Sermon on the Mount is actually a collection of topical teachings that Matthew compiled and set into a single delivery, it does not change the fact of the truth that He proclaimed everything that Father expects of His children. And in the end, because He spoke with such authority - more so than the established Scriptural experts of His day - the crowd of observers stood in awe and amazement, their minds quite figuratively blown away by this carpenter teacher from hicktown Nazareth.

Now three years later, after Jesus has invested His life into His closest allies, endured the betrayal of His friends and the shame and humiliation of the cross that took His life, He has once again risen in victory over death, Hell, and the grave. For forty more days, Jesus appeared to His followers and continued to teach them and prove to them that He had indeed been resurrected by the same power that had performed miracles for the previous three years. And He continued to declare the Kingdom of God and explain their part in it (Acts 1:3).

As once again, He stands on a mountainside outside of Jerusalem, overlooking the great city of God's immense affections, the question arises: "Is it now that You are restoring the kingdom of Israel?" And it is painfully evident that they still didn't understand. Israel has been oppressed under the boot of the Roman Empire and there was nothing they wanted more than freedom and restoration of their homeland. Now that Jesus had fulfilled the prophecy of a king riding into Jerusalem on donkey, they waited expectantly for the deliverance that was promised. Yet, the deliverance that was promised, was not the deliverance they expected.

"It is not for you to know times or epochs which the Father has fixed by His own authority." (Acts 1:7) Israel would indeed be restored as an independent kingdom. Israel would struggle back and forth for centuries between the Romans, the Byzantines, Christendom, the Mongols, and the Muslim Caliphates. In 1920, the British unfolded their plan to increase Jewish immigration to the Promised Land following World War I, and in 1948, Israel finally won her independence. But this was not the Kingdom that Jesus was speaking of.

"But you will receive power when the Holy Spirit has come upon you; and you shall be My witnesses both in Jerusalem, and in all Judea and Samaria, and even to the remotest part of the earth." (Acts 1:8) The Greek word for "power" here is "dynamis". It is the root word for many words in Latin and in modern English like "dynamite", "dynamic", and "dynasty". It is often referential of power in numbers or strength and influence. But its most common use is as a form of inherent power - a power that resides within by virtue of individual nature or temperament. It is referential to authority, more so than ability. This explains Luke's use of the word "martys" for Jesus' characterization of His disciples as "My witnesses." The word has carried with it some interesting connotations over the years, the most notable of which is being the root for the word "martyr." In reality, it is a legal term to describe someone who appears in court to testify to what they have seen.

Ultimately, yes, every one of the Apostles suffered persecution for the sake of God's Kingdom - a Kingdom that demands repentance and submission to God before the kingdoms of man. According to early church tradition, all of them were killed for their faith, except for John - who was boiled in oil and miraculously survived to be exiled on Patmos, where he received the final Revelation.

The Kingdom that Jesus has been teaching about all along was a Kingdom that is borne within the hearts of the repentant - the reborn. Jesus answered him [Nicodemus] and said "Truly, truly, I say to you, unless one is born again he cannot see the kingdom of God." (John 3:3) It takes new eyes and new ears to see and experience the Kingdom of God. It requires a renewed Spirit within us to guarantee our citizenship in the Kingdom. It requires God's stamp of approval and His empowering of us to be His ambassadors (2 Corinthians 5:20) in this world.

The Kingdom of God is established in the hearts of His followers and evidenced by the authority of the Holy Spirit living within us. It is demonstrated by our submission to His authority resulting in repentance. And it's an eternal battle - a battle that we cannot win on our own and by our own strength.

"For though we walk in the flesh, we do not war according to the flesh, for the weapons of our warfare are not of the flesh, but divinely powerful for the destruction of fortresses. We are destroying speculations and every lofty thing raised up against the knowledge of God, and we are taking every thought captive to the obedience of Christ, and we are ready to punish all disobedience, whenever your obedience is complete." (2 Corinthians 10:3-6)

The only way we can be a disciplinary force for change in society is to begin with ourselves. We must first "take every thought captive to the obedience of Christ." Then and only then do we have any right or authority to speak on behalf of the Kingdom of God in order to exact change in our world. To use the ways of the world to advance the mandates of the Kingdom of God is foolishness. Instead of using violence of the flesh to bring about a change of heart, we must learn the rules of engagement in spiritual warfare. Then and only then can we advance God's Kingdom in this world.

Reflection Questions

- Where do I still struggle to view the Kingdom of God as an inward reality before it is an outward mission?

  ____

  ____

  ____

- What thoughts, attitudes, or habits do I need to "take captive" to the obedience of Christ?

  ____

  ____

  ____

Application Points

- **Practice daily spiritual warfare through Scripture meditation**, asking the Spirit to expose and dismantle thoughts that oppose Christ's rule in your heart.

  ____

  ____

  ____

- **Identify one area where you have relied on human strength rather than Spirit-given power**, and submit that area to the Lord in repentance and obedience.

  ____

  ____

  ____

- **Ask God to renew your calling as His witness**, beginning first in your home and immediate relationships before extending outward.

  ____
  ____
  ____

Prayer Prompt

Lord Jesus, thank You for bringing me into Your Kingdom through the new birth and for giving me the power of the Holy Spirit. Teach me to take every thought captive and to fight the battles of life with Your strength, not my own. Shape my heart before You use my voice, and let my life reflect the authority and beauty of Your reign. Make me a faithful witness to the ends of the earth, beginning with the obedience You desire in me today. Amen.

Unity in the Kingdom

"Therefore if there is any encouragement in Christ, if there is any consolation of love, if there is any fellowship of the Spirit, if any affection and compassion, make my joy complete by being of the same mind, maintaining the same love, united in spirit, intent on one purpose." - Philippians 2:1-2

Unity does not equal uniformity. God has uniquely created and gifted you for a specific purpose within His Kingdom. We all have a role to play, but we all must learn what it means to synergize for the sake of the Kingdom. As a new creation in Christ, it takes time to renew our mind and restore our vision for the world around us. In the end, it is our love for Christ and our love for one another that must bind us together with a singleness of mind, heart, spirit, and purpose.

Unity of Mind

Unity of mind begins not with everyone believing exactly the same trivialities, but it does mean we are focused on the absolute truths of the essentials of our faith. Most specifically it means that we have an understanding of who Jesus is and that His authority overrules everything, even our own selfish desires. And that requires a new way of thinking about the world around us. It requires a new way of thinking about the people around us and how we ought to treat one another for the sake of the Kingdom.

"Do not be conformed to this world, but be transformed by the renewing of your mind, so that you may prove what the will of God is, that which is good and acceptable and perfect." - Romans 12:2

Unity of Heart

Unity of heart will only happen after we have experienced a renewal of the mind, but it is an ongoing process that will last as long as we are on this earth. When we "maintain the same love" for one another within the Kingdom, by extension we supernaturally extend that same love beyond the borders of the Kingdom. It's more than just a passing affection for one another, but it is love that must be maintained through pain and disappointment and discouragement and disagreement. When our need to be right becomes more important than our need to be in a right relationship with one another, we are no longer maintaining the same love for one another.

"Beloved, let us love one another, for love is from God; and everyone who loves is born of God and knows God. The one who does not love does not know God, for God is love." - 1 John 4:7-8

Unity of Spirit

Unity of spirit means getting deeper than the heart of the matter and recognizing that it is the Holy Spirit of God that must drive our decision making and our vision for the Kingdom. Not our own pet projects and causes. For too long we have begged and pleaded with God to bless the work of our hands. It is time that we start seeking the heart of the Father and earnestly seek out what God is doing in our world and join Him, because His work is already blessed.

"But I say, walk by the Spirit, and you will not carry out the desire of the flesh. For the flesh sets it desire against the Spirit, and the Spirit against the flesh; for these are in opposition to one another, so that you may not do the things that you please." - Galatians 5:16-17

Unity of Purpose

Unity of purpose will come only after we have experienced unity of mind, heart, and spirit. It takes renewed thinking, restored love, and reconciled spirit in order to full comprehend and contextualize the purpose that we have in unity for the Kingdom. Our purpose in this world is a very simple calling, but it is one that requires a proper mindset, a submissive heart, and Spirit-led discernment acting in unison with one another to fulfill. The advancement of the Kingdom of God is the fulfillment of the Great Commission - to make disciples. This is not a responsibility of simply the clergy, but rather it is the responsibility of the entire Body of Christ.

And Jesus came up and spoke to them, saying "All authority has been given to Me in heaven and on earth. Go therefore and make disciples of all nations, baptizing them in the name of the Father and the Son and the Holy Spirit, teaching them to observe all that I commended you; and lo, I am with you always, even to the end of the age." - Matthew 28:18-20

Advancing the Kingdom

The advancement of the Kingdom of God is made effective through a collective unity of mind, heart, spirit, and purpose. Paul's ministry of reconciliation (2 Corinthians 5:11-20) was all about building up the body of Christ so that each of us together can further the cause of the Kingdom. However, that requires that we understand what it means to be reconciled to God and to one another within the Kingdom before we do the work of expanding the Kingdom. The gifts and empowering of God in us are for the purpose of "equipping the saints for the work of service to the building up of the body of Christ; until we all attain to the unity fo the faith and of the knowledge of the Son of God, to a mature man, to the measure of the stature which belongs in the fullness of Christ." (Ephesians 4:12-13)

Reflection Questions

- Which area of unity (mind, heart, spirit, or purpose) do I most need the Holy Spirit to strengthen in my life right now, and why?

  ____

  ____

  ____

- Are there relationships within the Body of Christ where I need to pursue reconciliation or renewed love?

  ____

  ____

  ____

Application Points

- **Pray daily for a renewed mind** by meditating on Scripture, asking the Spirit to transform your thoughts and attitudes.

  ____

  ____

  ____

- **Take one practical step toward relational unity** this week—encouraging, forgiving, reconciling, or serving someone in the Body.

  ____

  ____

  ____

- **Identify one place where you can engage more intentionally in disciple-making**, whether through mentoring, teaching, or walking alongside a newer believer.

____

____

____

Prayer Prompt

Father, unite my mind, heart, spirit, and purpose with Your will through the power of Your Spirit. Form Christlike love in me so that I may walk in unity with my brothers and sisters in Your Kingdom. Equip me for the work of making disciples and building up the Body of Christ. Lead me toward maturity in the fullness of Christ, and use my life to advance Your Kingdom. Amen.

The Comfort of the Kingdom

"Rejoice in the Lord always; again I will say, rejoice! Let your gentle spirit be known to all men. The Lord is near. Be anxious for nothing, but in everything by prayer and supplication with thanksgiving let your requests be made known to God. And the peace of God, which surpasses all comprehension, will guard your hearts and your minds in Christ Jesus." - Philippians 4:4-7

During my childhood growing up in the 1970s and 80s in southeast Louisiana, it wasn't that uncommon that my mother would take me to the store with her every other weekend. Occasionally, we would drive all the way into Baton Rouge and visit the former Cortana Mall. Once situated in one quarter of the cloverleaf intersection of Florida Boulevard and Airline Highway, Cortana Mall was essentially the place to go when you went to the city. Across the highway used to be a bowling alley that my church youth group would frequent, where I once bowled better than a 200 (but only once.)

Being as we lived about 30 minutes away in the country, these trips to town back in those days often felt like a huge treat to get to experience a different side of life that we didn't experience daily in our quiet, serene lives in Pine Grove. On rare occasions as I got older, my mother would "release the leash" and let me roam the mall by myself or with a friend who was invited along in order to cure my boredom with perusing the giant clothing outlets.

However, as a younger child, I wasn't allowed to stray far from my mother's sight. And if I somehow wandered off and got lost, I would become fearful and cry out for her. Sometimes a store employee would see me and offer assistance with a kind smile in the hopes of calming my fears and anxieties until my mother could be located, usually only a few feet away.

Comfort in His Presence

Just as my mother was nearby and I was not out of her sight, in spite of my own blindness, our Abba Father is always near - His eyes ever watching and His hands ever guiding and comforting. Even when we can't see Him, He sees you. He rejoices over you in your victories and offers comfort in the midst of your pain. Just because you don't see Him in the midst of your darkness doesn't mean He shut off the lights. And when you experience pain and disappointment and discouragement, He is there offering a gentle hand of peace.

But all too often, because we become fixated on our circumstances, we lean on our own pride and humanity to pull us up by the bootstraps and push through the pain and the circumstances. Yes, it is true that God gave us a brain to use and think and reason with our situations, but sometimes, we reach a breaking point where the circumstance is beyond our competencies. Our natural response is to respond with fear or frustration or anger, which blind us to the comfort that is waiting for us if we simply stop and breathe Him in.

Comfort in Your Adoption

We can rejoice in knowing, no matter what circumstances we find ourselves in, the Lord is near, waiting for us to crawl into His lap to comfort us as His child. While our circumstances may exceed our competencies, His peace is capable of overcoming that beyond our own understanding. When we begin with the realization that the Lord is always near, we can stand in confidence knowing that even if we don't understand what is going on, His peace is readily available. He will help to guard your heart and mind and remind you of the grace and love He has for you as His child. Through Christ, you have been adopted into His family, and you belong to Him. You are not abandoned or forgotten — you are a beloved son or daughter of the King.

Let His peace reign in your heart and mind. Rejoice in the presence of the King of Creation! For you are an adopted son or daughter of the King of the Universe and He adores you. If you don't know Him, I urge you don't delay. He is waiting for you on pins and needles, longing for you to lift up your eyes and see Him for the truth that He is. While the door to the Kingdom is narrow, and path to the gate is difficult, the door is open to anyone who would walk through it. The rewards of Kingdom citizenship far outweigh the riches of this world.

If you want to know more about what it means to be part of the Kingdom, I'm just a quick click and an email away. There is nothing more important to me in this world than knowing that you know my Abba. If you don't know Him and want to know more, don't wait. Run! Peace to you, my friends, from the Father of all Creation.

Reflection Questions

- In what circumstances do I most often forget that God is near, and how does that affect my thoughts and emotions?

  ____
  ____
  ____

- Am I trying to navigate any present struggle in my own strength rather than placing it in the Father's hands?

  ____
  ____
  ____

Application Points

- **Pause in moments of anxiety** and pray Philippians 4:5–7, asking the Lord to guard your heart and mind with His peace.

  ____

  ____

  ____

- **Identify one fear or burden you have been carrying alone** and intentionally surrender it to the Lord in prayer this week.

  ____

  ____

  ____

- **Write down a Scripture about God's nearness** (Psalm 46:1; Isaiah 41:10; Matthew 28:20) and keep it visible as a reminder of His presence.

  ____

  ____

  ____

Prayer Prompt

Father, thank You for being near even when I feel lost or overwhelmed. Quiet my fears and help me rest in Your loving presence. Draw me close to Your heart, remind me of Your peace, and teach me to trust You in every circumstance. Make me confident in Your care and steady in Your love. In Jesus' name, amen.

The Touch of the Kingdom

"When he came down from the mountain, great crowds followed him. And behold, a leper came to him and knelt before him, saying, "Lord, if you will, you can make me clean." And Jesus stretched out his hand and touched him, saying, "I will; be clean." And immediately his leprosy was cleansed." - Matthew 8:1-3

There is power is the simple act of human touch; how much more so is the power of a touch from God! As Jesus leaves the mountainside following the sermon that has "blown the mind" of his audience, the crowd just can't get enough. They want more of this teaching and encouragement from this new teacher that shows them a way that even the current foremost experts of scripture of the day couldn't enunciate. Jesus spoke of seeking out God's kingdom and releasing our worries and that our Heavenly Father would pursue us and protect us and give us a foundation upon which to build a steady life.

Out of the midst of the crowd, with the rich and powerful still looking on from the sidelines, a man steps forward. Not just any man, but a man who was considered ritually unclean in accordance with the scripture as he had a debilitating skin disease. Leprosy was a highly contagious bacterial infection that easily passed from one person to another through touch from one infected person to another. It caused skin lesions and nerve damage, often leading to the loss of fingers, toes, eyes, nose, and other parts of the skin.

In the first century AD, people who contracted leprosy were confined to leper colonies and were forbidden to be in public. They were required to cover their faces and other parts of their bodies in order to not only hide their affliction, but also prevent spread of the contagion to others. This resulted in the stigmatization of an entire segment of society in the name of "public health". Lepers were routinely spit upon by the "clean" of society and shunned and pushed away, separated and left to die alone and abandoned.

Today leprosy is easily curable through proper treatment and sanitation, although in some parts of the world the cure in unavailable. Mother Teresa spent the majority of her life among this caste of "Untouchables" in India, ministering to the afflicted and the orphaned children wrought by this terrible disease. While today, leprosy is considered a very rare disease with fewer than 20,000 cases per year in the US, treatment requires medication and extreme sanitation measures. The disease is also spread by airborne droplets found in sneezes or other bodily fluids. And anyone who contracts leprosy will experience chronic pain for years after, if not for the rest of their lives. Sound familiar?

While the circumstances of COVID-19 were significantly different and statistically lower fatality rate among the afflicted, the societal response to it is no different. We treated people who we deemed a potential threat for not wearing a mask as "unclean". If anyone sneezes because of allergies, panic ensued. In some cases, people seemed to go out of their way to speak judgement against one another in the midst of this pandemic. The deaf and hard-of-hearing who were dependent upon lip-reading were especially isolated due to the loss of the ability to communicate with a world that already was silent to them.

I'm not suggesting that the public health measures that we instituted weren't warranted. However, we did reach a point in our society that we became isolated from one another as a people, afraid to even shake someone's hand or give someone a hug of comfort out of fear of contraction of a non-manifested disease or judgment from the authorities who governed those mandates. We effectively eliminated the power of human touch to lift up the lives of our neighbors.

Even today, we continue to be isolated from one another emotionally, physically, psychologically, politically, and ideologically – an isolation brought on by fear. Fear is a powerful motivator and is perhaps the most easily exploitable motivator in the human psyche as it paralyzes us and keeps us in a perpetual state of distrust.

But Jesus didn't care about the conventions of the day. A man stepped out of the crowd and mustered up the courage to ask the one person who had demonstrated His power and love to the crowds before teaching them on the mountainside to perform one more act of kindness - to touch him and make him clean. Imagine the gasps of horror escape the crowd as this diseased man approached Jesus. Obviously, there was even some apprehension within his own heart, because he asked "if you will, you can make me clean". There was some human doubt, but there was also trust in the divine power of Jesus to be able to heal him of his affliction.

From a human standpoint, leprosy was contagious and dangerous. Yet when Jesus touched the leper, there was no risk to Him in the way there would be for any other person. His holiness was never threatened, and His divine authority reversed the uncleanness rather than receiving it. In Scripture, the clean Jesus makes the unclean man clean — not the other way around.

And Jesus didn't hesitate as He stretched out His hand and touched him. He touched Him. A man afflicted with disease that naturally could have infected Him and His followers. He touched Him. But He didn't just touch His body; He touched His soul and heart. He healed not only His physical malady, but He healed his broken heart and loneliness and isolation. He restored his mind and gave him a reason to rejoice.

There is great power in graceful act of a kind touch from another human. A handshake. A fist bump. A warm hug from a friend. There is even more power when that touch is infused with the grace of God by the Spirit of God. It heals the heart. It releases the pain of loneliness. It increases the production of endorphins into the body - the happiness hormone.

While physical touch can indeed trigger the body's God-designed responses that bring comfort and calm, the deeper reality is that God often uses these simple, embodied acts of kindness to communicate His love. Human touch becomes a vessel of grace because we bear His image and His Spirit works through our acts of compassion.

Conversely, there is also great power in the violent act of an unkind touch from another human. When we strike one another in anger. When we withhold kindness and shrink away from one another in horror and fear. When we seek to destroy others instead of build them up. This creates pain and isolation. It destroys communities and divides nations.

If you want to see healing in your world, hug a friend. Shake the hand of a colleague. Kiss your spouse with passion. Give out of the goodness of your heart. Let the Spirit of God move you to be a neighbor that seeks the heart of God. Be a force for healing in our world. There is enough violence in the world without us adding to it out of fear and anger and bitterness of our own. But when seek the heart of the Father, it renews our mind and transforms our heart and gives us the strength to touch the hand and heart of our neighbors and families and friends. It gives us the ability to bring healing to the hearts and mind of those around us. Most importantly, it gives us hope for a brighter, healthier tomorrow.

Reflection Questions

- Where have fear, isolation, or self-protection kept me from offering Christlike compassion to others?

  ____

  ____

  ____

- How has Jesus touched my life in a place of brokenness, and how can I extend that same grace to someone this week?

____

____

____

Application Points

- **Practice a Spirit-led act of embodied kindness** this week: a handshake, a hug, a visit, or a word of

____

____

____

- **Ask God to reveal a person in your sphere** who needs the healing touch of compassion, and intentionally reach out to them.

____

____

____

- **Pray daily for renewed courage and love,** resisting fear-based withdrawal and embracing the calling to reflect Christ's compassion.

____

____

____

Prayer Prompt

Lord Jesus, thank You for touching the untouchable and drawing near to the lonely and afraid. Help me to walk in Your compassion, to extend Your love, and to overcome fear with the courage that comes from Your Spirit. Use my hands, words, and presence as instruments of Your grace. Renew my mind, soften my heart, and help me bring healing to those around me for the glory of Your Kingdom. Amen.

The Fulness of the Kingdom

A Concluding Meditation

"And when Jesus finished these sayings, the crowds were astonished at His teaching, for He was teaching them as one who had authority, and not as their scribes." Matthew 7:28–29

For forty days we have walked with Jesus up the mountain, listened to His words, felt the weight of His authority, and experienced the beauty of His Kingdom. We have seen that the Sermon on the Mount is far more than a collection of moral instructions. It is the portrait of a transformed people—a people shaped by the heart of the King.

Jesus has shown us that life in His Kingdom begins not with strength, but with poverty of spirit. It continues not through pride, but through mourning, meekness, hunger for righteousness, mercy, purity, and peace. He has prepared us for the reality of persecution and the joy of endurance. He has called us salt and light—His witnesses in a dark and decaying world.

He has taught us to pray, to forgive, to fast, to trust, to seek first the Father's Kingdom. He has warned us of false treasures, anxious hearts, hypocritical religion, and the wide road that leads to destruction. He has urged us toward the narrow gate, the firm foundation, the good tree, and obedience grounded in love. In all these things, Jesus is not merely giving commands—He is giving Himself. The Sermon on the Mount reveals the character of the King, and in beholding Him, we are changed.

A Kingdom Shaped by the King

Every virtue we have explored flows from the heart of Christ Himself:

- He is poor in spirit, choosing humility.

- He mourns over sin and brokenness.
- He is meek, yet mighty.
- He hungers and thirsts for righteousness.
- He is merciful to the undeserving.
- He is pure in heart – undefiled, unstained.
- He is the Peacemaker who reconciles heaven and earth.
- He is the persecuted One, the faithful Sufferer, the slain Lamb.
- He is the Light of the World, the true Salt, the solid Rock.

This is the invitation of discipleship – not mere admiration, but imitation; not mere inspiration, but transformation. The Sermon on the Mount is impossible apart from the grace of God, but radiant and beautiful when lived by the power of His Spirit. To follow Him is to be like Him.

A Kingdom That Cannot Be Shaken

When Jesus finished preaching, the crowds were astonished. They sensed authority in Him that exceeded anything they had ever known. That same authority now anchors your life. You belong to a Kingdom not built on sand, but on the unchanging Word of God. You belong to a King whose reign is eternal and whose promises never fail.

In a world marked by uncertainty, the Kingdom of God stands unshaken. And Jesus invites you – today, tomorrow, and every day—to build your life upon His words.

The Coming Kingdom has Arrived

The Sermon on the Mount is a foretaste of the world that Christ will one day restore. But it is also a picture of the life He empowers in His people right now. Every act of mercy, every peacemaking step, every quiet moment of prayer, every hunger for righteousness points forward to the day when the King returns and makes all things new.

Until then, you are His ambassador. You carry His light. You bear His name. You reflect His Kingdom in a world desperate for hope. Let the words of Jesus dwell richly in your heart. Let them shape your habits, your relationships, your priorities, your joys, and your sorrows. Let them guide you down the narrow path that leads to life. Let the King Himself be your treasure.

Reflection Questions

- As you look back over these forty days, what truths has the Holy Spirit impressed most deeply upon your heart?

  ____

  ____

  ____

- What next steps is Jesus calling you to take as a citizen of His Kingdom?

  ____

  ____

  ____

Application Points

- Choose one teaching from the Sermon on the Mount to intentionally practice this week—mercy, peacemaking, generosity, prayer, or purity of heart.

  ____

  ____

  ____

- Share with a friend, mentor, or small group at least one insight or commitment that emerged during this devotional journey.

  ____

  ____

  ____

- Consider rereading Matthew 5–7 in a single sitting to see the sermon again as a unified call to Kingdom living.

  ____

  ____

  ____

Prayer Prompt

King Jesus, thank You for speaking with authority, compassion, and truth. Thank You for calling me into Your Kingdom, forgiving my sin, shaping my heart, and giving me Your Spirit. Help me to walk in Your ways, build upon Your Word, and reflect Your light in a dark world. Make me a faithful citizen of Your Kingdom until the day I see You face to face. Amen.

www.ingramcontent.com/pod-product-compliance
Lightning Source LLC
LaVergne TN
LVHW010652110826
845149LV00014B/3055

* 9 7 8 1 3 2 6 3 0 1 0 1 9 *